MW00460810

"Mike Aquilina provides a historically accurate, theologically sound, and even exciting rendering of these early villains and their errors. Not only will you come to know the bad guys, but you will also come to know the heroes who helped to make all of us better Christians. A timely read."

—THOMAS G. WEINANDY, OFM, CAP.,
MEMBER OF THE VATICAN'S INTERNATIONAL
THEOLOGICAL COMMISSION

"Mike brings a wonderful ability of retaining historical accuracy, doctrinal orthodoxy, and modern application in a way unrivaled by most others."

—JOHN MICHAEL TALBOT,
FOUNDER, SPIRITUAL FATHER, AND GENERAL MINISTER
OF THE BROTHERS AND SISTERS OF CHARITY,
LITTLE PORTION HERMITAGE

"From the first to last, this book is a page-turner! Mike Aquilina takes his encyclopedic knowledge of the Church Fathers and Church history and presents a compelling explanation for the growth of Christianity."

—REV. FRANCIS J. HOFFMAN,
CEO/EXECUTIVE DIRECTOR, RELEVANT RADIO

"Aquilina provides a balanced, even sympathetic, portrayal of the tortured souls who thought they were doing divine work. This book is meticulously researched, yet beautifully accessible. Mike Aquilina makes the stories come to life in a fun, lighthearted, yet thorough presentation of the villains of the early Church."

—JIM L. PAPANDREA,
PROFESSOR OF CHURCH HISTORY AND HISTORICAL THEOLOGY,
GARRETT-EVANGELICAL THEOLOGICAL SEMINARY

"No one makes the early Christian authors more accessible than Mike Aquilina does. In these difficult times it is so strengthening to have the perspective that Aquilina provides for both scholar and layman. The Church has been through a lot, and her Lord has never left her."

—REV. RICHARD SIMON,
PASTOR OF ST. LAMBERT PARISH IN SKOKIE, IL,
AND HOST OF "FR. SIMON SAYS" ON RELEVANT RADIO

Villains of the Early Church

Villains of the Early Church

And How They Made Us Better Christians

MIKE AQUILINA

EMMAUS
ROAD
PUBLISHING

Steubenville, Ohio
www.emmausroad.org

Emmaus Road Publishing
1468 Parkview Circle
Steubenville, Ohio 43952

© 2018 Mike Aquilina
All rights reserved. Published 2018
Printed in the United States of America
Second Printing 2019

Library of Congress Cataloging-in-Publication Data

Names: Aquilina, Mike, author.

Title: Villains of the early church : and how they made us better Christians / Mike Aquilina.

Description: Steubenville : Emmaus Road, 2018.

Identifiers: LCCN 2018040562 (print) | LCCN 2018043856 (ebook) | ISBN 9781949013085 (ebook) | ISBN 9781949013061 (hard cover) | ISBN 9781949013078 (paper back)

Subjects: LCSH: Church history--Primitive and early church, ca. 30-600. | Enemies--Religious aspects--Christianity--Biography.

Classification: LCC BR162.3 (ebook) | LCC BR162.3 .A68 2018 (print) | DDC 270.1--dc23

LC record available at https://lccn.loc.gov/2018040562

Cover image: *Emperor Nero* (ca. 1618) by Abraham Janssens van Nuyssen, Caputh Castle, Schwielowsee, Germany

Cover design by Emily Feldkamp
Interior design and layout by Margaret Ryland

For Rosie

TABLE OF CONTENTS

ACKNOWLEDGMENTS

Kevin Knight (NewAdvent.org) and Roger Pearse (Tertullian. org) generously allowed me to use and adapt their patristic e-texts for this book. May God bless them abundantly. Most of the texts are from the nineteenth-century translations published in two series: *The Ante-Nicene Fathers* and *The Nicene and Post-Nicene Fathers.* Roger Pearse hosts some other rare translations at his remarkable site. I have taken the liberty of modernizing the English to make it more accessible to today's readers. When necessary, I have consulted the Latin and Greek originals, and sometimes have commissioned new translations. In footnotes I have simply referenced the work as it is most commonly known, along with the number of the section I've quoted.

Thanks to all those whose conversation and good humor keep me sharp, or at least less dull than I am by nature: my kids, their spouses, my grandkids; my siblings, their spouses, and my nieces and nephews; my colleagues and friends; and my parish priests at Holy Child in Bridgeville, Pennsylvania.

I credit my wife Terri for any good I do. She is the only life I know, and she is the reason my books get done.

Deo gratias.

INTRODUCTION

SUPERVILLAINS OF THE ANCIENT CHURCH

J*UDAS*: THE NAME itself means "traitor" now. In the story of
the Gospel, there are villains as well as heroes, and Judas is
the villain of all villains in the Christian story. Pilate the governor and Caiaphas the high priest are a close second and third.
The story has everything we love: a hero we can cheer and a pack
of villains we can hiss.

And the villains are essential. Without them, there is no
story. Without the evil, the hero never has the chance to be
good. Without Judas' betrayal, there is no Crucifixion—and
without the Crucifixion, there is no redemption. It's one of the
mysteries of evil: somehow the wickedest plots are the things
that God uses to save us from the wickedest plots. What we
intend for evil, God turns into good.

And in the story of early Christianity, it's often the villains
who give us the outlines. By a miracle of grace, they become
the occasions for Christianity to become more Christian. The

Church, faced with evil from the outside and inside, is forced to become more what it was always meant to be.

So here's something you don't see too often: a celebration of the villains in Christian history. Thank God for them, because we couldn't be Christian without them.

FOUR CENTURIES IN FIVE MINUTES

In four centuries Christianity grew from a tiny Palestinian sect to the dominant faith of the Mediterranean world. Along the way it had to face vicious persecutions, which were bad enough. But the enemies from within were harder to face.

The New Testament tells us most of what we know about the very beginnings of the Christian movement. We know the story of Jesus, the early days of the Church under the Apostles, and the travels of St. Paul. Already by the end of the Acts of the Apostles, the Church had started to spread to all nations, just as Jesus had commanded (see Matthew 28:19–20).

After that, we have thousands of pages of history to sort through.

As Christianity grew rapidly, it began to attract attention, and only about thirty years after the Ascension of Christ, the emperor Nero—one of Christianity's favorite villains—began the long series of persecutions that would continue for two and a half centuries. Now, with Christianity recognized as an illegal cult by the Roman authorities, we begin to have good eyewitness history from both inside and outside the Church, not just in bits and pieces, but in almost embarrassing abundance. Great Christian writers, such as Tertullian and Justin Martyr, tell us exactly what their church was like; pagan enemies, such as

Celsus, tell us what the scene looked like to educated and hostile Romans.

Some of the villains from this period are the notorious persecuting emperors. But this is also when we begin to see important heresies coming out—groups that call themselves Christian but don't believe what the great Church believes.

People often think of "orthodoxy" as the narrow line from which any deviation is heresy. This is wrong. The modern scholars who emphasize the diversity of early Christianity are right. Catholic Christianity was—and still is—a broad rainbow of different ideas, and most of the ones that were around in the earliest times are still with us. But Christians gradually had to draw lines to show where the broad field of Christianity ended and *something else* began. Orthodoxy was always a majority decision: the heretics were always in the minority compared to the Great Church—a term coined by the pagan anti-Christian writer Celsus to describe what was as obvious to him as it was to his Christian enemies.[1]

These heresies seemed—and were—dangerous at the time. But they were doing the Church a big favor. A Christian had to define more and more carefully what it meant to be a Catholic Christian. "In this way," said the great Latin theologian Tertullian, "even as the arguments of the opposing party are destroyed, our own explanations are being built up."[2] Or, as St. Augustine would put it later, "the fevered restlessness of the heretics stirs questions about many articles of the Catholic faith. But the need to defend them forces us to investigate them more accurately, understand them more clearly, and proclaim them

---

[1] Peter Lampe, *From Paul to Valentinus: Christians at Rome in the First Two Centuries* (Minneapolis: Fortress Press, 2003), 383.

[2] Tertullian, *Against Marcion* 5.6.

more earnestly. So the question raised by an adversary becomes the occasion of instruction."[3]

Even though Christianity was an illegal cult, the Church, according to the sociologist Rodney Stark, continued to grow for the first two and a half centuries or so at an astonishing rate of about 40% per decade.[4] Bursts of persecution produced heroic martyrs to inspire the faithful, but long intervals of relative peace allowed the Church to grow as an institution. The Roman government couldn't have hit on a better formula for spreading Christianity if it had tried.

By the year 312, Christians almost certainly made up the single largest religious group in the Roman Empire. That was the year everything changed: Constantine declared himself a Christian and won the empire under the banner of the Cross.

Now Christianity vaulted from illegal cult to the emperor's favored religion. But what was Christianity? Just as the faith had triumphed, an obscure priest named Arius brought the whole of it into question. Much of the next century would be taken up by the "Arian" question: is Christ really God, as the Church had always believed, or only a sort of deputy under-god called "God" by courtesy of the real God?

With one brief exception—Julian "the Apostate," who tried to revive paganism but found that rigor mortis had already set in—all the emperors after Constantine claimed to be Christian. That in itself created a new problem for Christianity. It was assumed in Roman government that the emperor controlled

---

[3] Augustine, *City of God* 16.2.

[4] Rodney Stark, *The Rise of Christianity: How the Obscure, Marginal Jesus Movement Became the Dominant Religious Force in the Western World in a Few Centuries* (San Francisco: Harper Collins, 1997), 7.

everything. But did he control the Church? It was an especially important question when the emperor was Arian.

Almost exactly a century after Arius, a bishop named Nestorius caused a new controversy that was almost as divisive as the Arian question. Was Mary Mother of God, or only Mother of the Christ? Once again, the Church was forced to define its long-held assumptions more carefully. By raising questions, a wrong teaching had given Catholic-Christian theology a good, hard shove.

Nestorius is perhaps the last great villain of the patristic age. Soon after his time, the ancient world fades into the Middle Ages. So we've just finished our five-minute tour of four centuries of Christian history.

But then there's Christian legend. And the villains in legend are at least as colorful as the villains in history.

LEGENDARY VILLAINS AND WHAT THEY TEACH US

Sometimes it's hard to sort out what's history and what's legend, but legend has its uses for the historian too. A legend may or may not preserve history, as in historical fact, but it does preserve a record of what people believed when the legend was current. Legend is a history of the mind.

For some of these legends, we dip into a class of literature called *apocrypha*, or sometimes *pseudepigrapha*. *Apocrypha* means "hidden things" in Greek, and it originally referred to concealed writings of secretive sects like the Gnostics. Since these writings were usually falsely attributed to some famous figure like an apostle, *apocrypha* soon came to mean "fake scriptures." In modern times, Protestants have used the term to refer to the books of the Old Testament that Catholics accept but Protestants don't. The term *pseudepigrapha* was invented by scholars to avoid all the confusion around the term *apocrypha*: it means writings falsely attributed to some author.

Many of these tales are quite colorful. You'll see how much trouble Judas and his wife had with chicken dinners that wouldn't stay put, for example. When people spend a lot of time thinking about characters in any story, they want to know more about them. It's only natural that the characters in the New Testament accumulated a lot of fan fiction. We can laugh at these stories now, but we shouldn't forget to ask ourselves what they mean. Why did people want to tell stories like these? What can we learn about Christian thought while we're laughing?

So, if you're ready, it's time to learn what we can from the most hated characters in Christian history and legend. And we're going to start right off with the most hated of them all: Judas Iscariot.

JUDAS

EVERYONE KNOWS the story of how Judas betrayed Jesus
with a kiss. Not everyone knows the story of Judas' home
life with Mrs. Judas and the trouble they were always having
with chicken dinners coming to life. For some reason those
stories didn't make it into the Bible.

THE JUDAS YOU KNOW

From the Gospels and the Acts of the Apostles we learn the few
facts we know about Judas Iscariot. He was the son of Simon
Iscariot (John 13:26), and they must have been fairly well-off
to be able to afford a last name that passed from father to son.

"Judas," or Judah (*Judas* is the Greek spelling of *Judah*),
was a very popular name in those days. It was the name of the
founder of the royal tribe of Judah, from which the kingdom of
Judah and later the province of Judea took their names. This was
also the name of the great national hero Judas Maccabeus. Furthermore, the word "Jew" was derived from the name. Simon

Iscariot must have thought he couldn't go wrong by naming his son Judas.

At least two of Jesus' disciples were named Judas: Judas Iscariot and Judas "not Iscariot," or Thaddaeus—our St. Jude. Ancient tradition tells us that Thomas was named Judas Thomas, which makes three.

The Gospels don't tell us why Jesus chose Judas Iscariot, or what made Judas decide to follow Jesus. We do know that, once he was among the Twelve, Judas took the job of treasurer. John tells us that he helped himself to the contents of the money box (John 12:6). Once again, it's a hint that Judas was from a higher economic class than the other eleven: they had picked him out as someone familiar with the handling of money.

We don't know much else about Judas' career as a disciple, but Matthew, Mark, and John all agree that the anointing at Bethany was a turning point for him.

The details of the story, which is in all four Gospels, are slightly different, but they seem to supplement rather than contradict one another. Matthew and Mark tell us that it happened in the house of Simon the Leper, Luke says this Simon was a Pharisee (Luke 7:36, 7:40). A woman brought a jar of very expensive ointment and anointed Jesus with it. Matthew and Mark tell us that the disciples were "indignant, saying, 'Why this waste? For this ointment might have been sold for a large sum, and given to the poor'" (Matthew 26:8–9).

John tells us that the woman was Mary, the sister of Martha and Lazarus. And he is more specific about which disciple was indignant:

> But Judas Iscariot, one of his disciples (he who was to betray him), said, "Why was this ointment not sold for

three hundred denarii and given to the poor?" This he
said, not that he cared for the poor but because he was
a thief, and as he had the money box he used to take
what was put into it. (John 12:4–6)

Jesus' response was clear: "The poor you always have with
you, but you do not always have me" (John 12:8; see also
Matthew 26:11; Mark 14:7). The woman had anointed his body
for burying, and she will be remembered for it wherever the
Gospel is preached.

And right after that Judas decided he had had enough.

Then one of the Twelve, who was called Judas, went to
the chief priests and said, "What will you give me if I
deliver him to you?" And they paid him thirty pieces of
silver. And from that moment he sought an opportunity to betray him. (Matthew 26:14–16)

What happened to Judas? Was it simple greed that snapped
him? That seems unlikely. Thirty pieces of silver was a good bit
of money, but Judas was doing all right with his embezzling
racket. The Gospels don't tell us his motivation most likely
because their writers just didn't know. It was a mystery to them
as it is to us. And a lot of the Christian legends that later grew up
about Judas seem like popular attempts to psychoanalyze him.

Judas was also present for the Last Supper, having a miserable time as Jesus told the disciples that one of them would
betray him: "The Son of man goes as it is written of him,
but woe to that man by whom the Son of man is betrayed! It
would have been better for that man if he had not been born"
(Matthew 26:24).

John tells us that the disciple whom Jesus loved—John himself—asked Jesus who the betrayer would be. "It is he to whom I shall give this morsel when I have dipped it," Jesus responded, and then dipped the morsel and handed it to Judas. Yet the others still didn't understand what Jesus meant when he said to Judas, "What you are going to do, do quickly" (John 13:26–27). Was he sending Judas out to buy more food? Or to make a donation to the poor from the money box?

"So, after receiving the morsel, he immediately went out," John says, adding the significant detail "and it was night." Judas walked out of the Last Supper and into the very symbolic darkness (John 13:30).

But he knew where to look for Jesus when he came with the police. Judas and the rest of the disciples had often been with Jesus in that pleasant park across the Kidron Valley, the garden of Gethsemane (see John 18:2; Mark 14:32). That was where Judas led the soldiers to arrest Jesus.

THE MISERABLE END

We get two versions of the end of Judas, obviously the same story, but differing in details. Matthew tells us that, after Jesus was handed over to Pilate, Judas "repented and brought back the thirty pieces of silver to the chief priests and the elders, saying, 'I have sinned in betraying innocent blood.'" When the priests responded "So what?" he threw the money at their feet and "went and hanged himself." The chief priests used the money to buy the plot of land since called the Field of Blood (Matthew 27:3–10).

In the Acts of the Apostles, Luke tells us that Judas bought the field with that money and "falling headlong he burst open in the middle and all his bowels gushed out" (Acts 1:18–19). This is how the Revised Standard Version Catholic Edition translates the passage, but the translators add a note saying that "falling headlong" could also be translated "swelling up," which will be the interpretation picked up by later Christian legend. Swelling up and bursting in the middle is the sort of thing that could happen to a hanged body in the Palestinian sun.

Thus, the accounts from Matthew and Luke agree on the essentials. The blood money went to buy the Field of Blood, and Judas came to a miserable end.

JUDAS AND CAIAPHAS

There's something deeply unsatisfying about the account of Judas in the New Testament. Why did he betray Jesus? We don't know—and maybe that's the point. We're all potential Judases. We could all betray the Lord for our own private reasons. We all *do* in the little sins we commit every day.

But we still want to know: what was going through his head? Was he angry that Jesus wasn't turning out to be the glorious military liberator he had imagined the Messiah would be? Was he hoping to provoke Jesus into action, maybe to start a rebellion against the Roman occupation?

When history leaves us with questions, legend steps in to give us answers. There are many legends about Judas, and most of them seem to be trying to answer the unanswerable question of why.

One legend that may be quite old or possibly medieval (it appears in a few medieval Greek manuscripts) has it that Judas was the nephew of Caiaphas the high priest, and Caiaphas had planted him as a mole among Jesus' disciples, "not to follow his teachings, but to betray him."[1] This answers the question of why Judas betrayed Jesus in a straightforward way: it was his job.

Other legends trace Judas' motivation to his home life with Mrs. Judas.

CHICKEN TROUBLE

Mrs. Judas is much abused in Christian legend. She often appears as the real motivator of Judas' betrayal. And for some reason she and her husband have a lot of trouble with chicken dinners.

In one Coptic story, Judas would take home the money he stole to Mrs. Judas. But, greedy as he was, he would sometimes cheat *her* of the money too. His wife, in this story, was the one who persuaded Judas to betray his Master.

An Ethiopian legend that used to be read on Maundy Thursday amplifies the story of the betrayal of Jesus. It begins in the house of Simon the Pharisee, where the anointing at Bethany took place. Simon's wife had just brought out a rooster that was cooked, cut up, and beautifully prepared and set it on the table in front of Jesus. When Jesus blessed the bread and offered it to Judas, Judas got up and left. Where was he going? It was easy enough to find out. Jesus healed the cooked rooster, which instantly hopped up, alive and well. Jesus gave it the gift of speech and sent it out to tail Judas as history's first poultry detective.

The rooster followed Judas back home, where it listened to the conversation where Mrs. Judas persuaded her husband to

---

[1] M. R. James, *The New Testament Apocrypha* (Berkeley, CA: Apocryphile, 2004), 161–62.

betray the Master. It tailed Judas as he went to the authorities and sold Jesus into their hands (one of those authorities, incidentally, was Paul of Tarsus). Then it came back to Bethany and told Jesus everything it had seen, weeping bitterly as it spoke.[2]

An ancient story that continued to be popular well into the Middle Ages tells how Mrs. Judas was cooking a rooster when Judas came home from throwing the blood money down at the feet of the priests.

"Wife," Judas said, "get me a rope. I'm going to hang myself."

Naturally, his wife asked him why he wanted to do that.

"I've betrayed my Master, Jesus, to the evildoers so they can hand him over to Pilate to be killed," Judas explained. "But he's going to rise again on the third day, and then we'll really be in trouble."

"Oh, come on," his wife said. "This rooster I'm roasting has as much chance of leaping up and crowing as Jesus has of rising again."

And of course at that moment the rooster jumped up, spread its wings, and crowed three times. Judas went and hanged himself.[3]

THE GOSPEL OF JUDAS

In 2006, *National Geographic* released the first published translation of the Gospel of Judas, a long-lost Gnostic text that had been recently discovered in one badly mutilated manuscript.

The massive publicity buildup promised that this new discovery would give us a radically different view of Jesus, and of

---

[2] James, *New Testament Apocrypha*, 150.
[3] James, *New Testament Apocrypha*, 116.

course it was hinted that everything we had been told about Christian origins was wrong. This is what always happens when some new manuscript discovery is made. And what unfailingly occurs when the discovery is actually published is that it confirms what we already knew about early Christianity. So it was with the Gospel of Judas.

Not that the Gospel of Judas isn't a valuable document. Any voice from the ancient past is priceless. But we had already known that Gnostics wrote such things. In fact, St. Irenaeus had told us before that he had seen a Gnostic "Gospel of Judas," which he summarized like this:

> They declare that Judas the traitor was thoroughly acquainted with these things [Gnostic doctrines], and that he alone, knowing the truth as no others did, accomplished the mystery of the betrayal. By him all things, both earthly and heavenly, were thus thrown into confusion. They bring out a fiction that they call Gospel of Judas.[4]

This sounds very much like the Gospel of Judas that was released in 2006 and that has since appeared in another more accurate translation.[5]

In the Gospel of Judas, the other eleven disciples all speak and act together, like the chorus in a Greek tragedy. They pray in their Jewish manner, and Jesus laughs at them for praying to their God, the God of the Old Testament. The disciples

---

[4] Irenaeus of Lyon, *Against Heresies* 1.31.1.
[5] Marvin W. Meyer, *The Nag Hammadi Scriptures: The Revised and Updated Translation of Sacred Gnostic Texts Complete in One Volume* (San Francisco: HarperOne, 2009), 760–69.

believe that Jesus is the Son of their God, which Jesus finds very amusing. The clear message is that ordinary Christians, followers of Peter and John and the rest, are deluded fools.

Only Judas, in this account, is willing to listen to the truth, so to him Jesus reveals the true Gnostic doctrines about the endless layers of aeons and angels and beings of light and luminaries and firmaments and heavens that make up the Gnostic universe.

But what about Judas himself? Is he hero or villain in this story?

It's hard to tell. That may be partly because the text is deliberately ambiguous. But it's also badly damaged. The most frustrating damage is exactly at the crucial point near the end, when Judas enters a cloud of light and the people on the ground hear a voice from the cloud saying something important. But that's exactly where the manuscript turns into confetti. We're not even sure if it's Judas in the cloud; it might be Jesus instead.[6]

After the cloud of light, Judas takes the money and betrays Jesus.

Was Judas doing what Jesus wanted him to do? Is Judas the hero of the story?

That's the way the publicity in 2006 portrayed him. It was certainly a sensational claim to say the most reviled villain in history turns out to be a hero of Gnostic enlightenment. But a closer reading of the story seems to suggest that Judas is more like a character from a Greek tragedy. Even though he's the only one who begins to understand what Jesus is teaching—even though he comes close to enlightenment—he betrays his Master. He's propelled forward by a destiny that's out of his hands.

---

6 Meyer, *The Nag Hammadi Scriptures*, 769n123.

In literary terms, the point of the Judas character in the Gospel of Judas is easier to understand. The other eleven disciples represent the ignorant masses who are too stupid to understand the "real" teachings of Jesus. Precisely because he's different from them and not part of their club, Judas can ask the questions that bring the Gnostic teachings out of the Jesus character.

The Gospel of Judas ends abruptly with the betrayal of Jesus—or rather of the man Jesus wears like a suit, since in Gnostic thought the real Jesus, who is spirit, didn't suffer on the Cross. We don't hear about Judas' end, and that very silence probably implies that we're supposed to understand that the rest of the story goes the way we know it from the Bible.

But other Christian legends were ready to fill the gaps left by Matthew and Luke.

The End of Judas

An old story ascribed to Apollinaris of Laodicea reconciles the details of the two New Testament accounts of Judas' death. Judas, he says, did hang himself, but he was cut down before he died. Then—and here Apollinaris refers to a lost book by Papias, who was a disciple of the apostle John—Judas swelled up so much that he couldn't go through a gate big enough to drive a chariot through and his eyelids puffed up until he went blind. Papias added further detail involving pus and worms that you definitely don't want to read before dinner. Judas lived on in that horrible condition for some time, but eventually he fell over and burst open, as we read in Acts, and to this day that field smells so horrible that you have to pinch your nose and hurry past.

A Coptic legend tells how Judas repented before Jesus was crucified and went to beg forgiveness from Jesus. Jesus told him to go out into the desert and repent, and to fear nothing but God. But in the desert, the devil appeared to Judas as a horrible monster and threatened to eat him up unless Judas worshipped him. Judas did—and then repented again.

But by this time Jesus was already dead. So Judas reasoned that the way to find Jesus was to kill himself and meet Jesus in the underworld, so he could ask forgiveness there. He did, but Jesus told him it was too late; he could not be forgiven for worshipping the devil and killing himself.

We'll see many more times that Christians like to imagine the worst villains as repenting in the end. But even the Copts, who gave us some of the most colorful legends in Christian tradition, couldn't quite imagine Judas successfully repenting.

Almost, but not quite.

CAIAPHAS

CAIAPHAS IS mentioned everywhere in the Church Fathers, but almost as furniture—"and Jesus was brought before Caiaphas." If the early Christian writers are interested in anything about him, it's that he could prophesy truly because of his office. Otherwise, they don't seem to find much remarkable in him. He's the banality of evil. A bureaucrat.

Yet, Caiaphas, like many of the characters caught up in the Passion story, was in a complicated position—more complicated than we may realize when we hear the story in the Gospels.

A DIFFICULT BALANCE

We get a hint of the complications when Luke, in his usual careful way, tells us exactly when John the Baptist began to preach: "In the fifteenth year of the reign of Tiberius Caesar, Pontius Pilate being governor of Judea, and Herod being tetrarch of Galilee, and his brother Philip tetrarch of the region of Ituraea and Trachonitis, and Lysanius tetrarch of Abilene, in the high-priesthood of Annas and Caiaphas . . ." (Luke 3:1–2).

The thing that stands out in this meticulous list is that there are two names of high priests. There's supposed to be one high priest, and the job is supposed to be for life. So why two names?

The answer has to do with the uneasy political relationship between the Roman government and the Jerusalem Temple authorities. The high priest had been Annas, but in the year 15 the Roman government had decided that Annas was too hard to work with. The Romans kicked him out and installed his son-in-law Caiaphas in his place. But many of the Jews believed that the Romans had no right to depose a high priest. They continued to recognize Annas as high priest. Luke simply describes the difficult political reality: two men were acting as high priest at the same time—one recognized by many of the faithful, and the other by the Roman government.

That was what Caiaphas had to work with. He was doing the official business of the high priest. He was the one the Roman government dealt with. But there were many people who ignored him and went straight to the old high priest. And to make things even more difficult, the old high priest was his wife's father.

Now we can make sense of John, who gives us the most detailed account of Christ's arrest and trial. "First they led him to Annas; for he was the father-in-law of Caiaphas, who was high priest that year" (John 18:13). But then in 18:19 John calls Annas the high priest. Even Jesus might well have been confused about who was interrogating him when Annas asked him what he had been teaching; Jesus replied that everybody had heard what he had taught in the open, so why was Annas asking him?

When he had said this, one of the officers standing by struck Jesus with his hand, saying, "Is that how you answer the high priest?" Jesus answered him, "If I have spoken wrongly, bear witness to the wrong; but if I have spoken rightly, why do you strike me?" Annas then sent him bound to Caiaphas the high priest. (John 18:22–24)

It's hard to make sense of this—the high priest sends Jesus to the high priest?—until we know about the peculiar political situation. Then we can understand. The faithful Jews wouldn't consider anything legitimate unless Annas had been involved in it. But it wouldn't be *official* without Caiaphas.

The conspiracy against Jesus seems to have been Caiaphas' idea. At least it was hatched in his palace (Matthew 26:3–4; compare John 11:47–49). Caiaphas was the one who told the bickering council, "You know nothing at all; you do not understand that it is expedient for you that one man should die for the people, and that the whole nation should not perish" (John 11:49–50).

You can see what he was thinking. Caiaphas had already spent more than a decade and a half keeping a delicate balance between the Temple priesthood and the Roman authorities. No street-preaching son of a carpenter was going to put his thumb on the scales. If something wasn't done, there would be riots and massacres. Caiaphas was not going to let that happen. He would not let the Roman authorities be challenged, and his own comfortable and prosperous position would be safe.

John knows that Caiaphas must have been thinking that way. But he's also sure that something else was going on. "He did not say this of his own accord, but being high priest that year he prophesied that Jesus should die for the nation, and not for the nation only, but to gather into one the children of God who are scattered abroad" (John 11:51–52).

Even when it was occupied by a scheming, petty bureaucrat like Caiaphas, the office of high priest came with the gift of prophecy. Caiaphas was a prophet whether he liked it or not.

Jesus and his disciples had known for a long time that his life was in danger in Judea (see, for example, John 11:7–8). But now the plot was in high gear. And Jesus and his friends seem to have had inside information about it: "Jesus therefore no longer went about openly among the Jews, but went from there to the country near the wilderness" (John 11:54). He was quite successful at hiding himself. As the Passover approached, the Temple authorities put out an all-points bulletin: "if any one knew where he was, he should let them know, so that they might arrest him" (John 11:57).

This is why the preparations for the Last Supper sound like something out of a spy novel: *go into the city, look for the man carrying a jug of water, and don't say anything—just follow him. Wherever he ends up, give the secret password, and you'll go upstairs and find everything ready for us* (see Mark 14:12–16).

And this is why the chief priests were so delighted when Judas came along. Without an insider to betray him, they might never catch this Jesus.

MANIPULATING THE GOVERNOR

Once Jesus was caught, the problem became complicated. Caiaphas had already decided that Jesus must die. At an overnight interrogation—we courteously call it Jesus' "trial," but there was nothing legal about it—Caiaphas satisfied the other

Temple authorities that Jesus was guilty of blasphemy. As far as they were concerned, that was a death-penalty offense. But they didn't have the authority to execute anyone. If they killed Jesus anyway, Pilate the prickly governor might call it a riot and have them all crucified. He was a touchy character, this Pilate. The only way to get rid of Jesus would be to manipulate Pilate into condemning him for crimes against Roman law.

Caiaphas, as the official representative of the Jewish establishment, had dealt with Pilate often enough to know which buttons to push. The thing Pilate feared most was getting in trouble with the emperor. If there were a riot, the emperor would want to know why. If there were an insurrection against the Roman government, the emperor probably wouldn't even stop to ask questions before relieving Pilate of his positions, and possibly his head.

So Caiaphas' strategy was to pin Pilate between a rock and a hard place. On the one hand, he brought crowds together to make it look as if a riot might break out if Pilate let Jesus go. On the other hand, he painted Jesus as an insurrectionist, ready to proclaim himself King of the Jews and lead a revolt against Rome. "If you release this man," the crowd shouted, "you are not Caesar's friend; every one who makes himself a king sets himself against Caesar" (John 19:12). It came from the crowd, but we can detect Caiaphas, the master manipulator, writing the script.

CAIAPHAS IN LEGEND

Caiaphas doesn't play a large role in early Christian legend. Pilate gets all the good parts. Caiaphas is usually just a bit player.

When he does appear, he usually plays the same function he takes up in the Gospels. He's the wicked schemer who sets plots against Jesus or the early Christians in motion. He orchestrates the conspiracy, assigning roles to all the minor players.

In one legend we already saw, for example, he had been plotting against Jesus from the beginning, planting his nephew Judas Iscariot as a spy among Jesus' disciples. The legend doesn't explain how Caiaphas knew Jesus was going to be dangerous way back at the beginning when Jesus was still in the disciple-picking stage, but perhaps it was that gift of prophecy working for him.

That same legend tells us that Caiaphas used his own daughter, Sarra, to make the false accusation against Jesus. Sarra, in the legend, was reputed to be a prophetess, so "all the Jews" believed her when she told them she had heard Jesus say that he could destroy the Temple and rebuild it in three days. Apparently, Caiaphas had a family of willing co-conspirators.[1]

As the young Church grew, according to the legends, Caiaphas still played the master manipulator. An early Christian novel known as the *Clementine Recognitions* has him summoning the Apostles for a debate. Caiaphas promises to listen impartially, like the humble seeker after truth he is. But of course he has no intention of being impartial. Once the debate is under way, he insults Peter as an ignorant fisherman and tries to shout down the Apostles. But of course the Apostles have the best lines. The main point is that Christianity is the true Jewish religion, the original faith that Moses established with the Ten Commandments; Moses' later laws were provoked by Israel's hardness of heart (see Matthew 19:8). Throughout the story Caiaphas is typically duplicitous, pretending to be interested in truth but actually trying to squash the Christians.

---

[1] "Story of Joseph of Arimathea," in James, *New Testament Apocrypha*, 161–62.

Christian legends like to provide appropriate ends for their villains. One old story has Tiberius arresting Caiaphas in a general sweep of all the people involved in the unjust execution of Jesus. But, once again, Pilate is the one we're interested in. The end of Caiaphas is appropriately ignominious. He dies in Crete on the way to Rome, so he doesn't even make it to his own trial. The earth refuses to take his body, so it finally has to be laid on top of the ground with a big pile of stones over it.

But let Christian legend go long enough, and it will find a way to redeem even the most hopeless villain. There's a Syrian tradition that Caiaphas eventually converted and took up missionary work. We don't know how old the story is, but the earliest evidence of it seems to come from 1222. It's a typically Christian legend: we just hate to leave Caiaphas out there unredeemed. We would rescue him—even him—if we could.

PONTIUS PILATE

J ESUS WAS crucified under Pontius Pilate. Countless millions of Christians recite that simple historical fact when they profess their faith. It reminds us that this is real history we're dealing with. The death and Resurrection of Jesus are not just metaphors or allegories: they really happened at a particular moment in history.

Pilate is our anchor to that historical moment. He is our grounding in historical fact.

But he's also one of the most fascinating characters in the Gospels. His doubt and dithering in the face of an unpredictable mob make him more than just a villain. They make him human, and we feel real sympathy for him. He's doing a bad job, but in his position it was nearly impossible to do a good job.

A Bad Place to Be Governor

The Roman province of Judea was one of the most troublesome places in the empire, and just a little historical background makes it easy to see why.

About 600 years before Pilate had to deal with the place, the kingdom of Judah was conquered by the Babylonian Empire. The Temple in Jerusalem was destroyed, the walls of the city were reduced to rubble, and the leading citizens were taken away to exile in Babylon. When Persia conquered Babylon, the exiles were allowed to return and rebuild, and for centuries they lived under Persian rule, which mostly left them alone as long as they paid their taxes and didn't make trouble.

After Alexander the Great conquered Persia, Judea became a battleground between two of the three great empires that succeeded Alexander's empire: the Ptolemys in Egypt and the Seleucids in Syria. The Books of the Maccabees tell us how the mad Syrian king, Antiochus Epiphanes, sparked a rebellion by trying to suppress the Jewish religion, and how the heroic Jewish resistance succeeded in establishing an independent Jewish state.

But one of the strategies the Maccabees used was an alliance with the up-and-coming power in the West, Rome. And once you came to Rome's attention, Rome didn't forget. By the time Jesus was born, Judea was a client state ruled by Herod the Great, who was more than a little mad himself, but who pretended to keep to the Jewish law even while he murdered his own family—which provoked Augustus Caesar's wisecrack that he'd rather be Herod's pig than Herod's son. When Herod died, Rome divided his territories, but took more direct control of Judea proper, the region around Jerusalem.

So Judea had a violent past and a population that hated being under the thumb of the vast and powerful Roman Empire. And their not-too-distant history gave them an example of a rebellion against another vast and powerful empire—a rebellion that succeeded. There were a lot of people in Judea who were ready to try again and see whether they could repeat the success of the Maccabees.

It was not an easy place to be governor. Not only were there constant threats from terrorists, but there was the strange religion itself to deal with.

Romans were used to respecting other people's religions. Your gods took care of you, and my gods took care of me, and we could all get along fine together. But the Jews had this strange idea that there was only one God—which was fine in itself, since many famous Greek and Roman philosophers had come to the same conclusion—but what set the Jews apart was their unwillingness to meet anybody else halfway. An educated Roman who believed what the philosophers said about the unity of God could still worship Apollo or Isis or whatever god happened to be popular wherever he was, on the grounds that these were all different expressions of the same divinity. But the Jews insisted that all the other gods were simply false and that it was evil to worship them. And their jealous God demanded that they keep to a whole system of laws of ritual purity. Anything an ordinary Roman did might somehow offend the Jewish fanatics, and then there would be riots.

And if there were riots, the emperor would want to know why. And Tiberius was not known as an easy boss to get along with.

All these things help explain some of what we see in Pilate's behavior: his uncertainty and fear of the mob, and his unwillingness to make any decision that would backfire on him.

But we also have Pilate's own character to deal with. He may have been dealt a bad hand, but how he played it was his own fault.

ARE YOU THE KING OF THE JEWS?

The first question Pilate asked Jesus was a question designed to find out what sort of troublemaker he was. "Are you the King of the Jews?" (Matthew 27:11; John 18:33). If the answer was yes, Pilate would know what to do. It would mean that this Jesus was yet another in the long line of would-be rebel leaders claiming to be the expected Anointed One, the Messiah. As Pilate had heard it from his Jewish informants, this Messiah was supposed to be a conquering hero who would destroy Roman power and restore the independent Jewish state. If that was who Jesus claimed to be, Pilate could have him executed as a rebel and go back to his interrupted breakfast.

But when Jesus told him, "My kingship is not of this world," Pilate knew he wasn't dealing with an ordinary rebel (John 18:36). Jesus might be crazy, but he wasn't dangerous. So why were the Temple authorities insisting that Jesus must be killed? What had he done to offend them? Pilate must have realized with a sinking feeling that he was about to end up knee-deep in one of those Jewish religious disputes that nobody but Jews could understand.

And it couldn't have helped his mood when a message came from his wife: "Have nothing to do with that righteous man, for I have suffered much over him today in a dream" (Matthew 27:19). Even the most enlightened and educated Romans could be very superstitious, especially about things like dreams.

As if that weren't enough, the chief priests had put him in a deliberately uncomfortable position. They couldn't come into the governor's residence to see Pilate, so they had made Pilate come out to see what they wanted. It was one of those ritual-purity things, but it was also a not-very-subtle reminder that they could make Pilate's job very hard for him if they liked. Every time he wanted to talk to the people who had brought Jesus to him, he had to go back out to the front porch (see John 18:28–29, 18:38, 19:4).

The different Gospels give slightly different details of the encounter between Jesus and Pilate, but they all agree on the main point: Pilate didn't want to have anything to do with this problem and did everything in his power to fob it off on somebody else. He repeatedly asked the crowds to let him release the prisoner as his usual Passover courtesy to the natives, but they insisted that they wanted Barabbas instead (John 18:39–40). He told the chief priests to take care of it themselves, but they said they wanted him killed, which they weren't allowed to do themselves (John 18:31). When he found out that Jesus was a Galilean, he happily threw the whole problem into the lap of Herod, the ruler of Galilee (son of Herod the Great). But the problem bounced right back (see Luke 23:6–11). He tried to get Jesus himself to explain what was going on, but Jesus just talked a bunch of nonsense about "truth." "What is truth?" Pilate asked (John 18:37–38). It might make a good epitaph for him.

Every time Pilate tried to release Jesus, the mob looked more riotous. The chief priests simply would not accept the idea of releasing Jesus. It had cost them a lot of trouble to catch him: this was their one chance to kill him, and they weren't going miss it.

Pilate dithered quite a bit. He scourged Jesus, on the grounds that anyone who was taking up the valuable time of the Roman governor at least deserved that much, and then tried to tell the crowd yet again that he found no crime in Jesus. When the mob wouldn't accept that, Pilate again tried to get an answer out of Jesus, but Jesus wouldn't admit to anything that deserved the death penalty. Pilate tried to release Jesus again, but the chief priests played their trump card: "If you release this man, you are not Caesar's friend" (John 19:1–12). Finally Pilate literally washed his hands of the whole business, declaring that he was innocent of Jesus' blood. But he wouldn't stand in the way of a crucifixion if that was what the mob wanted (see Matthew 27:24–26).

Nevertheless, Pilate couldn't resist one sarcastic insult to the Jewish authorities who had backed him into this corner. Over Jesus' head he put the inscription that marked the criminal's crime: "Jesus of Nazareth, the King of the Jews" (John 19:19).

Surely the chief priests understood the insult. "Do not write, 'The King of the Jews,'" they told Pilate, "but, 'This man *said*, I am King of the Jews'" (John 19:21).

"What I have written I have written," Pilate replied, and the Cross stood with his original inscription (John 19:22).

After that, Jesus was out of the way, and Pilate probably figured he had avoided another riot and could now enjoy some peace and quiet. When Joseph of Arimathea asked for the body, Pilate was willing to give it to him—what harm could there be in that? (See John 19:38.) And when the chief priests asked Pilate for a guard to keep Jesus' disciples from stealing the body, he gave them what they wanted, because it made them go away (Matthew 27:62–66). This is the last we hear of Pilate in the Gospels.

PILATE IN OTHER HISTORIES

But Pontius Pilate is a well-documented character in history, in the New Testament and in the works of other writers. Archaeologists have even found an inscription from a building dedicated when he was governing Judea, and his name written in stone somehow makes him seem all the more real to us.

Other historians paint the same familiar character we know from the Gospels. According to Philo of Alexandria, Pilate was corrupt, cruel, and prone to exceeding his authority, even—to no one's shock—to the point of executing prisoners who had yet to be condemned. According to the famous Jewish historian Josephus, Pilate did try to work with the Temple authorities, but had no understanding of—or interest in—Jewish law.

Pilate is obviously the same character in these histories that we see in the Gospels. He had a genius for doing the wrong thing at the wrong time. He was cruel when patience would have kept the peace, and he was indulgent when he ought to have been firm—as, for example, when he allowed Jesus to be crucified because he was afraid of a riot.

Josephus and Philo also tell us the historical end of Pilate. He was governor for ten years and did a very bad job of it. In the year 36, he was recalled to Rome, charged with going beyond his authority, provoking riots, and persecuting the Jews. According to Philo, Pilate was believed to be unusually corrupt even by the notoriously corrupt standards of Roman governors. Thus, his career ended in disgrace.

But his career in legend had just begun.

Pilate in Legend

In apocryphal legends, Pilate often plays the role of the impartial judge, forced by the facts to acknowledge the divinity of Jesus. Most of these legends, after all, grew up as Christians attempted to convince the people around them of the facts of the Incarnation, and a few corroborating details were always welcome.

There's a long composition called the *Acts of Pilate* that exists in many different versions in various languages. The majority of it, in most versions, purports to be a more detailed record of Pilate's encounter with Jesus. There are many interesting details left out of the Gospel accounts: for example, when Pilate sends for Jesus by messenger, the messenger, having heard the acclamations on Palm Sunday, lays a cloth in front of Jesus so that he can enter like a king (which infuriates the Jewish authorities), and when Jesus does enter, all the carved busts on the Roman standards bow in reverence. That impresses Pilate, and it's exactly then that his wife sends him the message about her dream. In the *Acts of Pilate*, Pilate's wife is a God-fearer, a Gentile who worships the God of the Jews, so her dream should have some authority with the chief priests. But their answer is that Jesus is a sorcerer, which explains the standards and the dream, because sorcerers can do that sort of thing.

Pilate examines the charges further and is shocked to find that Jesus is charged with healing on the Sabbath. "They want to put him to death for a good deed?" In a long trial, various followers of Jesus present testimony in his favor: Nicodemus tells of his many signs and wonders; Veronica tells how she was healed by touching the hem of his garment; the blind and the lame who are now whole give their evidence.

After hearing all this, Pilate is furious with the chief priests, reciting a short history of the unfaithfulness of the Jews to their God ("according to what I've heard"), and is about to release Jesus. But the mob backs him into the corner we expect to find him in by painting Jesus as the enemy of Caesar and adding that this is the king that old King Herod was looking for when he killed all those children. That is enough to put the fear of Caesar into Pilate, and he washes his hands and proceeds as in the Gospels.[1]

Legend also has provided some of Pilate's official correspondence with Rome. In some manuscripts of the *Acts of Pilate*, Pilate privately interrogates Annas and Caiaphas, who admit that, yes, the Scriptures do show that Jesus was the Son of God. Since Pilate has already executed Jesus and has heard that he's now walking around very much alive, he's naturally disturbed. He writes a letter to the emperor (Claudius, for some reason—a bit of an anachronism) telling how he had been duped into executing the Son of the God of the Hebrews, who has since risen again.[2]

In other traditions, Pilate corresponds with the emperor Tiberius, explaining how he came to execute the righteous Jesus; there is also correspondence between Pilate and Herod, in which Pilate tells Herod that "this is all your fault."

There's a legend that Mary Magdalene, furious at the execution of the Lord, went to the emperor Tiberius himself and told him what Pilate had done. This is said to be the reason for Pilate's recall in disgrace.[3]

---

[1] See "Acts of Pilate," in James, *New Testament Apocrypha*, 94–103.

[2] "Acts of Pilate," in James, *New Testament Apocrypha*, 144–46.

[3] James, *New Testament Apocrypha*, 117.

In most of these legends, especially the ones from the West, Pilate can't be forgiven. He had the Son of God before him, and he failed to prevent the Crucifixion. Though he had private scruples, they simply show his lack of courage—he failed to act on them. When Tiberius has him beheaded, we feel that he richly deserved it.

But there's a very different tradition in some parts of the East.

SAINT PILATE?

In Coptic and Ethiopian churches, Pontius Pilate is a saint and a martyr. He bore witness to the divinity of Christ, as did his wife Procla. In one such story, when Pilate is about to be beheaded, he hears a voice from heaven: "All generations and families of the Gentiles will call you blessed, because all these things that were spoken by the prophets about me were fulfilled in your time. And you will be my witness at the Second Coming, when I judge the twelve tribes of Israel and those who have not confessed my name."[4]

It's interesting that Christians felt a maternal tenderness toward Pilate and the others who had brought about Jesus' death—a truly motherly mercy. Maybe they knew that Caiaphas and Pilate were stand-ins, doing the work of every sinner—*of every one of us*. They wished them well and wished it ardently.

Though our scanty historical records—the Gospels and a couple of other historians—suggest that Pilate was a miserable ditherer to the end, we can hope that he repented, that he saw what had really happened in the strange events surrounding the

---

[4] *Paradosis Pilati*, 10.

death of the prisoner he had crucified under protest. We can hope that those Eastern churches are right. We can hope that we'll meet Pilate in heaven.

SIMON MAGUS

I F THERE had been supermarket tabloids in Rome of the first century, Simon Magus, or Simon the Magician, would have been on the front pages every week. His story gives us zombies, levitation, a talking dog, a jewel heist, and a prophesying baby, just to name a few of the highlights.

But it all begins with a true story in the Acts of the Apostles.

SIMONY

The story takes place in "a city of Samaria"—we're not told which one—where Philip the deacon had gone to preach the Gospel. Philip healed many and freed many from evil spirits. "So there was much joy in that city."

> But there was a man named Simon who had previously practiced magic in the city and amazed the nation of Samaria, saying that he himself was somebody great. They all gave heed to him, from the least to the greatest,

saying, "This man is that power of God which is called Great." And they gave heed to him, because for a long time he had amazed them with his magic. But when they believed Philip as he preached good news about the kingdom of God and the name of Jesus Christ, they were baptized, both men and women. Even Simon himself believed, and after being baptized he continued with Philip. And seeing signs and great miracles performed, he was amazed. (Acts 8:5–13)

When the apostles Peter and John showed up, they confirmed the new Christians by laying hands on them, so that they received the Holy Spirit.

Now when Simon saw that the Spirit was given through the laying on of the apostles' hands, he offered them money, saying, "Give me also this power, that any one on whom I lay my hands may receive the Holy Spirit." But Peter said to him, "Your silver perish with you, because you thought you could obtain the gift of God with money! You have neither part nor lot in this matter, for your heart is not right before God. Repent therefore of this wickedness of yours, and pray to the Lord that, if possible, the intent of your heart may be forgiven you. For I see that you are in the gall of bitterness and in the bond of iniquity." And Simon answered, "Pray for me to the Lord, that nothing of what you have said may come upon me." (Acts 8:18–24)

The story gives its name to the sin of "simony," which is the attempt to purchase the gifts of the Church with money. The text makes it clear that Simon himself knew he wasn't "somebody great." He was as "amazed" by Philip as people of the city had been by Simon. And as a practicing magician, he was probably used to the idea that magic was for sale. Perhaps he thought the Apostles had the real magic he himself had been faking.

In Acts, after Peter rebukes him, Simon appears to repent, and Luke gives us what looks like a happy ending to his story.

But in Christian legend, Simon became one of the chief villains. And although the Simon traditions are legendary, they're very ancient. We can't dismiss them out of hand just because we don't have DNA evidence. Allowing for a lot of exaggeration and wide-eyed credulity, there seems to be a real historical character behind the stories.

THE ARCH-HERETIC

For most of the early Christian writers, Simon Magus is the arch-heretic from whom all other heresies are derived. The legends give us a pope-versus-antipope scenario, Simon Peter versus Simon Magus, highlighting the singular status of Peter. And the drama, of course, moves from the Holy Land to Rome.

Simon Magus is usually depicted as a Gnostic, the founder of Gnosticism. And we do know of an early sect of Gnostics who called themselves Simonians and apparently traced their secret doctrines back to Simon Magus.

How much of the rest of the story is true you can judge for yourself.

According to the ancient writer St. Epiphanius, Simon Magus fell in love with a slave prostitute named Helen, and he built his Gnostic mythology around her and their relationship. He was God (no one in the stories ever accuses Simon of false modesty). She was his *Ennoia*, his "First Thought," who had been trapped in the material world in an endless cycle of reincarnations. She had been all the famous beauties of history, including (of course) Helen of Troy. Now God had come in the form of Simon to rescue her from her material prison—and he could do the same for you.[1]

Like other Gnostics, Simon believed that matter was evil. In his mythology, matter was created not by God but by the angels, who had all rebelled.

The *Acts of Paul*, a book that Tertullian says was written not long before his time (so probably in the middle 100s), tells us that these were the main points of Simon's teaching:

1. There is no resurrection of the flesh, but only of the spirit.
2. Human bodies were not created by God.
3. God did not create the world and does not know it.
4. Jesus only appeared to be crucified.
5. Jesus was not born of Mary or of the line of David.[2]

So far Simon sounds like a typical Christian Gnostic thinker. But in legend he was most famous as a magician whose amazing illusions led even faithful Christians astray.

SIMON VS. SIMON

In the *Acts of Peter*, a kind of fantasy novel written (probably) in the late 100s, Simon Magus has a big part. The story tells us

---

[1] Epiphanius, *Panarion* 21.3.5.
[2] See "Acts of Paul," in James, *New Testament Apocrypha*, 289.

that he was a wonderworker who claimed that his power came from God: "he was a great power of God, and without him God did nothing."[3] So he wasn't God in this version, but God's right-hand man. He even had some of the Christians fooled: "Is not this the Christ?" they asked each other.

As we find out later on, Simon was in Rome because he had to leave Judea in a hurry. He'd been living in the house of Eubula, a rich woman who was wowed by Simon's parlor tricks. Eubula had a large collection of jewels, and of course they attracted the wicked Simon's attention. With two accomplices to help deal with the loot, he used magic to take away the jewels. And he would have gotten away with it, too, except for an interfering amateur detective who had an unfair advantage.

The detective was Peter, of course, and he used the power of prayer to identify the fence who was trying to dispose of the jewels. The jewels were recovered, the heist was exposed, and Simon had to run from an angry mob.

Told in a vision that Simon, the Power of Satan, had gone to Rome, Peter set off to confront him. Thus, in the story, Simon Magus provides the motivation for Peter's move to Rome.

In Rome, as we know, Peter found that many of the Christians had fallen for Simon's illusions. With an inspiring speech, Peter reconverted them, and they begged him to fight against Simon, who was claiming to be the "power of God."

Simon was staying at the house of Marcellus, a Christian senator who had fallen for Simon's act. This Marcellus had once been noted for his charity to widows, orphans, and the poor. It had gotten him in trouble with the emperor, who was angry that Marcellus was spending his money on vile persons, instead

---

[3] "Acts of Peter" in James, New Testament Apocrypha.

of giving it to worthy recipients such as, just for example, the emperor. But once under the spell of Simon Magus, Marcellus immediately repented of his earlier charity and, after that, he sent poor strangers away with a beating.

(For early Christian writers, the very mark of a heretic was lack of charity. Our anonymous author is hitting us over the head with it: as soon as you abandon orthodox Catholic Christianity, all your charity evaporates.)

Peter went to the house of Marcellus and asked the servant who answered the door to tell Simon that Peter was there to see him—"Peter, because of whom you ran away from Judea," just to make sure he got the point.

But Simon had already heard that Peter was in town. "He told me to tell you he's not in," the servant replied.

This was not going to stop Peter. He looked around and spotted a big dog chained nearby, so he let the dog off the chain. And the dog immediately spoke: "What do you want me to do, servant of the ineffable and living God?"

"Go in and tell Simon to come out," Peter told the dog. "Tell him I came to Rome specifically to see him, the wicked deceiver of souls."

So the dog ran in the house and found Simon spewing his Gnostic nonsense to Marcellus and his household. It stood up on its hind legs and delivered Peter's message verbatim.

Well, that was something you didn't see every day. Simon was speechless. But Marcellus was convinced by the talking dog that Peter must be the real apostle. He ran out to Peter, fell at his feet, and begged Peter to pray for him. He confessed that he had been so much taken in by Simon that he had even put up a statue to him inscribed "To Simon, the New God." Simon had deceived him by teaching that Christ had taught a secret knowledge that Peter and the other disciples did not understand. (This is the basic tenet of all Christian Gnosticism: that there is a secret teaching of Christ that's only for special people like you.)

Meanwhile, Simon was in the house arguing with the talking dog, as Peter learned from a young man who had a demon in him. Peter cast out the demon—but as the demon was leaving him the young man broke a statue of Caesar. Marcellus was distraught: this was treason, and heads would roll. But Peter told him to calm down and prayed for the statue to be healed, and instantly the statue was as good as new, which certainly impressed Marcellus.

Back in the house, Simon was still arguing with the dog: "Tell Peter I'm not here!"

The dog, having run through all Peter had told it to say, was now improvising. "Here I am, a dumb animal sent to you with a human voice to confound you and show that you're a deceiver and a liar, and the best you can come up with is 'Tell Peter I'm not here'? Aren't you ashamed of yourself?"

Having cursed Simon thoroughly, the dog turned and went back out to Peter, with all the people in this house (except Simon) following to see what would happen. The dog reported all it had said and Simon's replies, and prophesied, "Peter, you will have a big showdown with the enemy of Christ, and you will turn many back to the faith." And then it died at Peter's feet.

By this time there was quite a crowd gathered around Peter. "Show us another one," some of them said, and Peter obligingly reanimated a dried herring that was hanging in a window nearby. The revived fish became a tourist attraction, and people would throw bits of bread into the water and watch it eat to prove it was alive.

Some time later, Marcellus threw Simon out of his house. So Simon, in desperate straits (and furious over the beating Marcellus and his servants had given him on the way out) ran to the house where Peter was staying and challenged him: "Here I am, Peter! Come down and I'll prove to you that you've believed in one who was a Jew and a carpenter's son."

Peter, though, did not deign to appear himself. Instead he found a woman in the house who had a seven-month-old baby and told her. "There's a man downstairs who wants to see me. Go down to him, but you don't have to say anything to him. Just wait and listen to what your baby tells him."

As soon as the woman and child reached Simon, the baby spoke in a man's voice: "Son of a shameless father! You never put out your roots for good, but only for poison. You weren't even confounded when a dog rebuked you. Now here I am, a baby, compelled by God to speak, and you're still not ashamed! But on the next sabbath you'll be brought into the forum of Julius to show what kind of man you really are. And now, Jesus Christ tells you, 'Be dumb in my name, and leave Rome until the next sabbath.'"

And Simon was immediately struck dumb, and he left the city and stayed in a stable.

After a few days (which Peter filled with miraculous healings and other signs), the time of the big showdown arrived. The enterprising Romans had set up bleachers in the forum and were selling tickets. And the spectators would get their money's worth.

The confrontation began as a religious debate. Simon's argument (is it perhaps an echo of the arguments of the real Simonians?) was that Jesus' birth records are available. He was a carpenter and the son of a carpenter. "Is God born? Is he cruci-fied? If he has a master, he isn't a god."

But the audience wanted signs and wonders. The prefect would act as judge. His challenge: Simon must kill a slave without touching him, and Peter will resurrect him. Simon killed the slave with a word in his ear; Peter raised the boy, and a widow's dead son for good measure. Simon moved a dead senator by a bit of sorcery, but Simon's resurrection was just a fake—a reanimated corpse with no real life in it. Peter revived the senator to real life.

Peter was clearly the winner. But Simon did not take his defeat lying down. He tried to revive his reputation with sham miracles, but they were all tricks. His healings and resurrections were temporary. He was a vaudeville act.

At last, desperate to revive his fortunes, Simon challenged Peter again. This time he gave a demonstration of his most spec-tacular trick: levitation. And (with the help of demons, as later versions of the story elaborate) he pulled it off. Huge crowds gathered to see him flying high above the city.

But Peter prayed to God that Simon would fall and break his leg in three places, and Simon fell and broke his leg in three places. Once again, the real power of God beat the sham power of Simon's magic. And in this version of the story, Simon died, not from the fall, but from going to a doctor to have his leg set. If he had repented, it is doubtless that Peter could have taken care of it for him. But he was still too proud to trust in God.[4]

---

[4] "Acts of Peter," in James, *New Testament Apocrypha*, 306–32.

What Simon Magus Means

These are wild stories, and no one today would take them seriously as history. But although the stories themselves don't qualify as history, they do tell us a very important historical fact.

The fact is this: Simon Magus was one of the great bugbears of early Christianity. Christians in the first few centuries knew that someone by that name had existed and that he was in some way the enemy of everything they stood for. And he was an enemy of the worst kind: an enemy who came from inside the Church. To the first writers on heresies, all heresies could be traced back to Simon Magus, the father of heresies. And we do know that the early Gnostics operated just the way we see Simon Magus working in these stories. They didn't make converts of pagans or Jews. They preyed on the converts the Catholic Church had already made.

Because of Simon's position as the father of heresies, it may never be possible to reconstruct what he actually taught. In a sort of religious novel called the *Clementine Recognitions*, for example, we once again get the story of Peter confronting Simon Magus—but this time the contest is a theological debate. And Simon's ideas seem to be Marcionist, suggesting that the author is using a well-known first-century villain to attack Marcion, a figure of the second century.

Nevertheless, there is a strong overlap between the claims Simon makes about himself in the *Clementine Recognitions* and in the other stories about him. Simon is a power above the Creator: "I am the Messiah, and I am called the Standing One." He calls himself the "Standing One" because "I am indissoluble." And he's famous for his magic tricks: invisibility, boring through mountains, flying, escape artistry, animated images, and turning into a sheep, among many others. Again, we see parallels with the *Acts of Peter*.

According to St. Justin Martyr, Simon had a disciple named Menander who continued his deceptions, including claiming divinity.[5] St. Irenaeus traced the Gnostic heresies all back to Simon.[6]

Whatever the historical facts about him, Simon Magus was a very real villain in the minds of early Christians. Justin Martyr made a bit of a fool of himself by actually asking the Roman Senate to pull down a statue of Simon he had found on the island in the Tiber. He read its inscription as *SIMONI DEO SANCTO* ("To Simon the Holy God"), which certainly reminds us of the statue Marcellus had put up in the *Acts of Peter*. Actually, Justin knew very little Latin—since Rome had a huge Greek-speaking community, it was quite possible for him to live there without learning the language. In fact, the Christian liturgy was in Greek during his time, even in Rome. If Justin had known his Latin better, he might have read the inscription more accurately. Such statues have actually been found, including on the Tiber Island, with the inscription *SEMO SANCUS DIUS FIDIUS*. They're dedicated to the old Sabine god of oaths.[7] But Justin's mistake shows how thoroughly he believed the Simon Magus stories he had heard.

We've already heard one story of the death of Simon Magus. Apparently there's no authorized version, and many other stories exist. According to Hippolytus, whose story is as good as anybody's, Simon told his followers that if he were buried alive, he

---

[5] Justin Martyr, *First Apology* 26.

[6] Irenaeus, *Against Heresies* 1.23.1.

[7] See Lampe, *From Paul to Valentinus*, 269.

would rise again on the third day. They buried him, and he's still there.[8]

---

8 Hippolytus of Rome, *Refutation of All Heresies* 6.15.

NERO

PILATE WAS A waffling dupe. Judas was a tortured soul who didn't have the courage to repent. But perhaps no villain in Christian legend comes out as completely and utterly villainous as Nero. He isn't just a sinner who made the wrong choice: in much of Christian legend, and even theology, he is literally the Antichrist.

A NOT-VERY-BLESSED EVENT

To be fair, most of the pagan writers who tell us about his life hate him as much as the Christians do. Nero is the great villain of Roman history, the symbol of everything that could go wrong with the imperial system. And the wrongness begins before he was born.

Nero's father, Gnaeus Domitius, was a kind of Dickensian villain. The ancient historian Suetonius (who gives us much of our information about Nero) calls him "a wholly despicable character." Domitius once killed a freeman (a former slave) for refusing to drink the absurd amount Domitius had told him to drink. Once when driving down the Via Appia, the great Roman superhighway southeast of the city of Rome, he deliberately accelerated his horses to run over a random boy he saw in a village because he thought it would be an amusing thing to do. He was charged with treason, adultery, and incest, and those are just the highlights.[1]

Surprising as it may seem, Domitius managed to find a wife who was almost his equal in vice: Agrippina, who would later become notorious as her son's partner in crime and teacher in vice.

Nero, their son, was born—very appropriately—just a couple of days before Saturnalia, the Roman holiday when the world turned topsy-turvy. Saturnalia was a midwinter carnival in which slaves got to play the role of masters and masters played at being slaves, and everyone tried to outdo everyone else in silly practical jokes. According to the story that was always told about his birth, it happened just at sunrise, and the rays of the sun touched the newborn boy just as he was being laid on the floor.

The Romans, you see, had a ritual at birth. The newborn child was laid on the floor, and if the father acknowledged it as his child, he took it up in his arms. But if he didn't—if it was defective somehow, if it was missing a limb or turned out to be a girl or had some other terrible defect—then he turned away from the child, and it was thrown out with the garbage.

Domitius did acknowledge his new son. But he made an amusing prediction about the boy, perhaps even a prophecy.

---

[1] Suetonius, *Life of Nero* 5.

"Any child born to Agrippina and me," he said, "is bound to be a menace to society."[2]

When Nero was three, his father died, and the whole estate was seized by Nero's uncle, Gaius, known to history as the mad emperor Caligula. Agrippina and her boy were banished for being too closely related to the emperor to be safe to have around, and Nero spent some time being poor (and probably resentful) during what modern psychologists might call his formative years.

But when Caligula died suddenly, the intellectual Claudius succeeded him. Claudius restored the confiscated estate, and Nero and his mother were now very rich. Things took an even brighter turn for the boy when Claudius adopted him at the age of eleven or twelve.

From a poor exile, Nero had now come to be next in line to the imperial throne.

As a tutor for his young successor, Claudius hired the very best: Seneca, the Stoic philosopher and famous rhetorician. The night before he began his duties, Seneca had a strange dream that his young pupil was really Caligula come back to life. Romans put a lot of faith in dreams—but what could Seneca do? You don't refuse the emperor.

At fifteen, Nero was married to Octavia, the daughter of Claudius, to shore up his claim to the throne even more. And then at sixteen, he suddenly became emperor.

A Pretty Good Emperor

Claudius died very suddenly after eating a plate of mushrooms. The rumor that was almost universally believed was that Agrip-

---

[2] Suetonius, *Life of Nero* 6.1.

pina had gotten tired of waiting for Claudius to pass on by natural causes and had decided to get him out of the way with poison. Mushrooms were Claudius' favorite dish.

There was extravagant mourning for Claudius, and the Senate declared him a god—something that was within the Senate's authority, though its authority over earthly things had mostly vanished with the rise of the emperors. Privately, Nero said that mushrooms must be the food of the gods since Claudius became a god by eating them. This was the sort of thing that tickled his sense of humor.

Nero, meanwhile, had no illusions about who was responsible for his elevation. On the day he became emperor, he gave the military tribune on duty his new password: "best of mothers."

In spite of the dubious circumstances, Nero began his reign as a pretty good emperor. Suetonius tells us that he "never missed an opportunity of being generous or merciful or showing what a good companion he was."[3] He lowered taxes and gave 400 sesterces each to the people of Rome. Wherever he went he always remembered names and faces; he had the natural politician's gift of picking someone out of the crowd whom he had seen once before and making that person feel like his best friend.

And it wasn't all just buttering people up. Nero made wise reforms in government. When he judged a case, he insisted on deliberating in private and having the arguments written up so he could study them. He cracked down on government corruption, and even the Nero-haters among the historians had to admit that, at least early in his reign, he did manage to clean up the government quite a bit. (This brief portrait of Nero's childhood and early reign is taken mostly from Suetonius.)

---

[3] Suetonius, *Life of Nero* 10.1.

"I have assembled this catalogue of Nero's acts—some forgivable, some even praiseworthy—in order to segregate them from his follies and crimes, which I must now begin to list."[4] So writes Suetonius as he turns to what the pagan historians considered the most atrocious aspects of Nero's reign. And of all the atrocities Nero committed, Suetonius decides to deal with the music first.

THE NERO SHOW

The thing upper-class Romans could never come to terms with about Nero was that he really wanted to be a performer more than an emperor. They were hoping for a wise ruler; Nero wanted to be a rock star. And the more the upper classes hated his performances, the more Nero hated the upper classes.

Nero had always loved music, and soon after he became emperor he took up lyre-playing and singing lessons. It's usually said, that is, that Nero played the lyre, but the historian Richard C. Beacham suggests that Nero probably played the cithara, not the lyre. This is even more horrifying because the cithara was a professional's instrument, meant for public performances. Whichever instrument, it was bad enough that Nero was learning to sing and play like some sort of cafe singer-songwriter. But then he started performing in public.[5]

The historians tell us that Nero was never very good at his lyre-playing and singing. But then that's the sort of thing they would say as good upper-class Romans, who believed that any sort of public performance by the emperor denigrated their

---

[4] Suetonius, *Life of Nero* 19.3.
[5] Richard C. Beacham, *Spectacle Entertainments of Early Imperial Rome* (New Haven, CT: Yale University Press, 1999), 212.

whole class. For a writer like Tacitus, admitting that Nero was any good at all would have been like a Jew saying, "I think Adolf Hitler was a pretty good painter." Even if you had a thought like that, you'd keep it to yourself.

We do know that the common people—the dregs of society, as Tacitus would have thought of them—applauded Nero wildly when he performed. He certainly took his vocal training seriously, and there's some evidence that he may have impressed a handful of the critics.[6] It's hard to tell. On the one hand, the historians who are our main sources have their prejudices; and on the other hand, when you're emperor, no one tells you to your face that you stink.

At any rate, cities in Greece, where the performing arts were a long tradition, began "sending him every available prize for lyre playing," according to Suetonius.[7] They didn't actually have to hear him; the fact that he was emperor was good enough for them. Soon, Nero began public recitations of his poetry as well. Although the upper classes sneered as usual (Tacitus thought Nero's poetry was lousy), Suetonius had some of Nero's original manuscripts to look at, and he honestly admitted that he thought the poems were pretty good.[8] Of course the fawning Senate went a good bit further than that: Nero's poems were "printed in letters of gold on plaques dedicated to Jupiter Capitolinus."[9]

None of that flattery was good enough for Nero, who honestly sweated over every performance. Suetonius tells us that he was in awe of the judges, even though the judges knew

---

[6] Edward Champlin, *Nero* (Cambridge, MA: Harvard Belknap, 2005), 57.
[7] Suetonius, *Life of Nero* 22.
[8] Beacham, *Spectacle Entertainments*, 198.
[9] Suetonius, *Life of Nero* 10.

that there would be huge rewards for them if Nero earned a prize. And he worried incessantly about the audience, even though the audience was in his pocket. In fact, he had hired a squadron of more than five thousand young men to learn the showy Alexandrian styles of applause to use at his public performances, and with cheerleaders like those leading the way, he was sure to get a rousing ovation. Certainly no one walked out on him, for the simple reason that there were guards stationed to make sure no one left during his performances. "We hear of women in the audience giving birth and of men being so bored with the music and applause that they furtively dropped down from the wall at the rear or shammed dead and were carried away for burial."[10]

Even when Nero wasn't the performer, there was no missing his presence. He made a place for himself at the theater, directly over the stage. He didn't just watch the show: even when other actors were performing, Nero was the show.

Besides singing, recitation, and acting, Nero took up chariot racing as well. Again, he took it very seriously. At one race he fell out of his chariot, but he ran to catch up with it and managed to get back in and drive some more. Even though he didn't finish the race, he was still awarded the prize. Again, our historical sources mock Nero and the fawning judges, but to be thrown from a chariot and then to recover enough to take up the reins again shows some serious skill, not to mention determination.

Nero's reign turned into an endless succession of spectacles. He revived an old play called *The Fire*, which featured a real fire in his production, and just to make the performance

---

[10] Suetonius, *Life of Nero* 23.5.

more realistic, the actors were allowed to keep whatever valuables they could rescue from the flames. He staged a chariot race with chariots drawn by four camels, because it was something new and different. One show featured elephants on tightropes. There was a naval battle on an artificial saltwater lake with "sea monsters" swimming in it. There were even gladiator shows in which, by special command of the emperor, no one was allowed to be killed. And in many of these shows, senators or equestrians—the cream of the upper classes—were forced to perform for the common people.

In fact, the world seemed to be in a permanent state of Saturnalia. Nero the populist was turning society upside-down. The proud were humbled, and the humble exalted; the last the first, the first the last. Nero promised his plebeian base exactly what Christ had promised his followers. But Nero would give it to you right now. And it was a hellish mirror image of the promise of Christ: in Nero's world, the plebeians would finally have their chance to outdo the aristocracy in vice.[11]

It's worth pointing out that the upper classes who hated Nero—the senators, equestrians, and decurions—made up less than 17% of the empire. They wrote our histories, but there are many indications that the vast majority of common people in the empire had a very different opinion of Nero. Just in Italy, for example, 40% of the population was enslaved, according to the best modern estimates. The emperor who made a permanent Saturnalia out of Roman life must have been very much to their taste.[12]

---

[11] Champlin, *Nero*, 149–51.
[12] See Lampe, *From Paul to Valentinus*, 172, 186.

NERO THE MONSTER

As it became more and more clear to Nero that he could get away with anything, he found more things to get away with. The list of his personal crimes is appalling even by the atrocious standards of Roman emperors. It was widely rumored that he had an incestuous relationship with his mother, and Agrippina was certainly the sort to use any kind of leverage she could get to keep herself in a position of influence. It didn't help in the end, though: like most of Nero's favorite people, Agrippina had to go eventually. He had her killed, and then spent much of the rest of his life worrying about her avenging spirit.

Nero was devoted to his second wife, Poppaea, who was by all accounts a great beauty. But something happened one day. He kicked her to death in a fit of rage. He never got over her death—and the death of their unborn child, since she had been pregnant at the time. He found a mistress who looked very much like Poppaea. Then he procured a boy who looked strangely like Poppaea and had him castrated, after which he went through a wedding ceremony with the mutilated boy. When he played female characters in his tragic recitations, Nero always wore a mask carved in Poppaea's likeness. (In fact, Nero had a particular taste for characters who had killed family members—Orestes the matricide, Oedipus blinded, Hercules raving, and so on.)

Another sham wedding had Nero playing the blushing bride, "and on the wedding night he imitated the screams and moans of a girl being deflowered."[13] This seems to have been a piece of what we would call performance art or, perhaps more

---

[13] Suetonius, *Life of Nero* 29.1.

accurately, an elaborate practical joke. But it was typical of Nero's taste in humor.

Nero not only developed his own vices to an unusual degree: he also encouraged vice in everyone around him. He believed that all people were really just as full of vices as he was, so anyone who confessed to the most outrageous kinds of obscenity would be forgiven any other crime.[14] Chastity, in Nero's opinion, was always a lie.

Suetonius tells us that Nero held all religions in contempt, but we should probably make one exception. He was very keen on the cult of himself. That old story about the rays of the sun striking him just as he was born seemed to him to mean that he was himself associated with the sun god Apollo. Images of Nero show him with the rays emanating from his head that usually marked Apollo in pagan iconography, and in inscriptions he is called the New Apollo, or Nero Apollo, or Apollo Augustus.[15]

Naturally, an emperor who portrayed himself as a god incarnate would strike the Christians in Rome as particularly devilish. But Nero would give them even better reasons to hate him.

NERO VS. CHRISTIANS

There were already quite a few Christians in Nero's time. Tacitus tells us that the Jews had caused disturbances "at the instigation of Chrestus," which almost certainly refers to the disputes between Jewish Romans and the Christians, who were indistinguishable from Jews to the Romans' eyes during the beginning of Christianity. "Chrestus" was a familiar Greek name, and it

---

[14] Suetonius, *Life of Nero* 29.
[15] Champlin, *Nero*, 116–17.

was how the Romans commonly heard the name "Christus" even more than a century later, as Tertullian remarks: "Which you corruptly pronounce 'Chrestians.'"[16]

Since the Christians were mostly foreign (the Christian liturgy in Rome was in Greek for at least the first two hundred years), mostly poor, and mostly harmless, the Romans naturally hated them. It seems there was already a lot of anti-Christian feeling in Rome by Nero's time. And if there's one thing a populist like Nero finds extremely useful, it's a hated minority to use as a scapegoat.

It didn't take long for Nero to need a scapegoat. In July of 64, a fire broke out in Rome. The flames spread so rapidly that all attempts to fight them were futile. By the time it burned itself out days later, most of the best parts of the city were in ashes.

This was a calamity that needed decisive action and, to his credit, Nero reacted quickly, making sure the homeless had shelter and doing what he could to keep the city going.

But there was also a rumor that Nero himself had set the fire. It was certainly true that, almost as soon as the embers stopped glowing, Nero was at work on a vast palace complex that would replace much of what formerly had been the best part of the city. The story that he had picked up his lyre and started to sing about the fall of Troy while the city was burning seemed very much in character. People were rapidly passing from shocked to angry: they wanted someone to blame.

Well, if the people wanted somebody to blame, Nero would give them somebody to blame. *Look*, he pointed out: *the Christians believe that the end of the world is coming, and haven't you*

---

[16] Tertullian, *To the Nations* 1.3.

heard them say that the world will end by fire? And, look, the neighborhoods where most of the Christians live (the poor neighborhoods, where Nero didn't plan on building any palaces) *were spared by the fire. And, look, you already hate the Christians. Therefore, obviously, the Christians started the fire. They probably wanted to hurry the end of the world along. Don't you hate those Christians?*[17]

So Nero put on his biggest show yet: the Let's-Kill-the-Christians Show.

> They made fun of them while they died. The Christians were killed by wrapping them in animal skins and having them ripped to shreds by dogs, or they were crucified or burned. When day was done, they were set on fire as nocturnal illuminations. For this spectacle Nero opened his gardens and put on a circus game, mingling with the people in a charioteer's garb, or standing in a chariot.[18]

This is how Tacitus describes Nero's surreally sadistic den party, in which the common people of Rome, still reeling from the destruction of the city, were invited to relax and enjoy some healthy torture and murder. In fact, this seems to be the occasion Nero chose for his debut as a charioteer.

Tacitus himself seems to be appalled by the cruelty, and he talks as though everyone else was appalled too. "Therefore," he continues, "even though these people were guilty and merited the worst punishment, they were pitied. People seemed to think

---

[17] See Lampe, *From Paul to Valentinus*, 47.
[18] Tacitus, *Annals* 15.44.

they were being destroyed not for the good of the community, but for one man's bloodlust."[19]

But Suetonius, who follows a categorical rather than chronological scheme in his biography, lists Nero's punishment of the Christians among the *good* things he did. And in spite of the sadism of the punishments, they were actually penalties with precedent in Roman law. Crucifixion, as we know, was a standard practice. Arsonists were in fact liable to burning, which suited the ancient Romans' idea of balancing the scales of justice. And even being sewn up in animal skins and torn by dogs was not one of Nero's clever inventions, but actually a standard punishment in Roman law for certain crimes.[20] It may well be that Nero's punishments were quite popular among the lower classes—there were, after all, crowds of people for him to mingle with, and they must have showed up to enjoy the show. It would be almost impossible to overstate the sadism of the Roman public. Perhaps the thing that really irritated Tacitus was not the barbarism of the punishments, but the fact that, once again, Nero was appealing to the common people's love for colorful spectacles, rather than acting like the decent and tasteful upper-class emperor Tacitus would have preferred.

According to ancient tradition, Peter and Paul both died during this first official Roman persecution of the Christians. Peter was crucified (upside-down at his own request, because he was unworthy to die the same death as his Lord); Paul, a Roman citizen, had the privilege of being beheaded rather than crucified.

It's easy to see how this orgy of torture would not have made Nero the Christians' favorite among the emperors. But it

---

[19] Tacitus, *Annals* 15.44.
[20] Lampe, *From Paul to Valentinus*, 82–83.

was worse than just a few days of mad violence. Nero's persecution established the principle that Christians were dangerous to society. Roman law had taken no notice of Christians as a specific group before the Great Fire. Now they would be an illegal sect, subject to the death penalty if discovered. Nero wasn't just the first persecutor; he was the author of all the future persecutions.

And that raised Nero to a higher position than anyone else in the pantheon of Christian persecutors. He wasn't just a bad man: for many Christians, Nero was the Antichrist himself.

Nero as Antichrist

In the mythology that some Christians developed around Nero, he would return at the end of the world. He would be either the Antichrist from the Book of Revelation or the Beast, who would in turn be defeated by the real Antichrist, and then he in his turn would be defeated by Christ. Many of the Christian writers of the time were dubious about this popular belief, but the Nero-as-beast idea at least has some pretty clear support from Scripture itself. The number of the beast in Revelation is 666—the number of the name NERON CAESAR spelled out in Hebrew letters, which are also used as numerals. Augustine was doubtful about the idea of Nero as Antichrist; he was surprised people would be so presumptuous as to make such speculations. But the fact that he had to address the subject more than three centuries after Nero's death shows how durable the legend was.

Perhaps it was not so much Nero's persecution as his popularity that suggested him for the role of Antichrist, for the idea that Nero would return from the dead did not originate with the Christians. It was an idea they picked up from the pagan world around them. Throughout the Roman Empire, there were people who believed that Nero would return, even centuries after his death. And his return would be a great day for the common people.

But if he really did return, he would be a nightmare for the Christians.

THE END OF NERO

Nero might have been very popular among ordinary people, but it was the kind of popularity that was bankrupting the Roman Empire. There was no way an emperor could keep up the kind of lavish spending Nero kept up. And the more he spent, the more Nero soaked the upper classes, resorting before too long to false accusations against rich Romans so that their estates could be confiscated.

The upper classes, used to holding all the power, were bound to fight back eventually. When even the Roman soldiers felt that they couldn't trust Nero, it was inevitable that they would rebel.

And when the rebellion started, it's not surprising that the leader dwelt not on Nero's cruelties, but on his embarrassing performances. The soldiers were used to the idea of an emperor who led them to glorious victory in battle, or—at the very least—rewarded the generals who led them to glorious victory, so that the rewards seeped down to the common soldiers. They didn't have much respect for an emperor who had no interest in military affairs at all.[21]

The leader of the ultimately successful rebellion was a general named Vindex. He dwelt on the indignity of having a man on the throne who played the roles a common actor would

---

[21] Beacham, *Spectacle Entertainments*, 251.

play, who acted as a singer and a herald instead of an emperor. "Is there anyone who will call a man like that Caesar, Emperor, Augustus? Never! Those titles were sacred."[22]

And all the soldiers who listened to him agreed: no, Rome can't have an emperor who thinks of himself as an artist. That's not what emperors do.

The rebellion started in Gaul, and by the time the news of it reached Nero it was already a dangerous force. But Nero refused to take it seriously. In fact, he made a big show of not taking it seriously. He called his advisers together for what they thought would be a conference on the emergency—and then announced that he had invented a new and improved water organ that was both louder and more musical than current organs. He would soon demonstrate it, he said—"if Vindex kindly gives me permission."[23]

But when the Gallic uprising became too serious even for Nero to ignore, the emperor prepared an expedition. Or, rather, he prepared a road tour for the Nero Show. There would be a wagon just to carry his costumes and props. He had a plan: he would perform the tragic role of the Betrayed Emperor in front of the soldiers, which would win their hearts, and then they would all sing victory songs that he would compose for them.

Somehow this plan never came to fruition. The governor of Spain, Galba, had thrown his support behind the rebellion, and the legions in Africa had rebelled too—Africa, where most of Rome's grain supply came from. The people of Rome were quickly turning against Nero now that the bread supply was interrupted. When Nero finally decided he wasn't safe in the

---

[22] Cassius Dio, *Roman History* 63.22.5.
[23] Cassius Dio, *Roman History* 63.26.1.

city anymore, he found that his Praetorian Guard—the emperor's own bodyguard—wouldn't follow him if he ran away. He ran away anyway, taking his boy-wife—the one who looked like Poppaea—with him. The Senate declared Nero "Public Enemy Number One" (now that he was down, the senators were lining up to kick him).

Nero set out for Ostia, but he was closely pursued. There would be no escape. Finally, he realized that suicide was his only dignified option. "Such an artist," he said—"and I'm dying!"[24]

Nero was only thirty years old when he died. The upper classes threw a big party, running around the streets wearing freedman's caps, as if they had just been released from slavery. But not everyone was delighted to see Nero go. "The dregs of the city . . . the scum of the slave population"—these, according to Tacitus, were the people who mourned Nero. In other words, ordinary people.[25]

Certainly the Christians among the ordinary people weren't big fans of Nero—although there is one curious legend that has Nero executing Pilate for his unjust execution of Jesus.[26] More typical of the Christian view, however, is the story in the *Acts of Peter* in which Nero has a vision of someone scourging him and telling him he can't persecute the Christians anymore. He stops the persecution and there is much rejoicing.[27]

But the legend of Nero went on. Even centuries later, there was a sort of underground hope in some places that Nero would reappear. False Neros, like false Messiahs, suddenly came out of nowhere and gained large followings before finally being put

---

[24] Cassius Dio, *Roman History* 63.29.
[25] Beacham, *Spectacle Entertainments*, 253.
[26] Champlin, *Nero*, 28.
[27] "Acts of Peter," in James, *New Testament Apocrypha*, 336.

down by the Roman authorities. (One of the qualifications for pretending to be Nero seems to have been that you had to be a passable lyre-player.)[1]

How late did these Nero legends survive? No one can really tell; they were legends passed down among ordinary illiterate people. But in the year 1099, more than a thousand years after Nero died, we get a hint that they were still circulating. In that year, Pope Paschal II built what is now the Church of Santa Maria at the Piazza del Popolo in Rome. It was built on what was believed to be the site of Nero's tomb, and the pope built it specifically to exorcise Nero's evil ghost.[2]

So Nero died at the age of thirty, but his ghost lingered in Rome for at least a thousand years.

---

[1] Champlin, *Nero*, 57.
[2] Beacham, *Spectacle Entertainments*, 254.

MARCION

"And there's Marcion, a man from Pontus, who's still alive today. He teaches his disciples to believe in some other God greater than the Creator. And with help from the devils he's caused many people of every nation to speak blasphemies and deny that God is the maker of this universe, saying that some other who is greater than he is has done greater things."

— Justin Martyr, *First Apology* 26

MARCION WAS A rich businessman who thought he had figured out the real meaning of the Gospel. He used the power of money to found a kind of parallel church, and he was very successful for a while—which tells you a little about the state of Christianity at the time, and a lot about what you could do with money in the Roman Empire in those days.

Marcion was born at some time in the 80s, according to

the best guess scholars can make.[1] He came from Pontus, way out on the Black Sea, and his opponents loved to paint Pontus as the wild East, a barbarian land of cannibals and female warriors. But their sources were centuries out of date. Pontus was quite civilized in Marcion's time. It had been taken into the Roman Empire in Nero's reign, and it had all the usual Roman conveniences.[2]

From what little we know of his writings and arguments, we can guess that Marcion probably had the equivalent of a high school education, perhaps with a concentration in math and astronomy. He was educated, but not what we'd call an intellectual.[3] Like most Easterners, he spoke Greek.

He first appears in history when he showed up in Rome in about 140. He had already made a pile of money, because he happened to have picked one of the best businesses for making piles of money at the time.

Marcion was a shipping magnate, with at least several ships plying the Mediterranean trade routes. Because the whole economy of the empire depended on shipping huge quantities of stuff from here to there, the imperial government made sure the ship owners were well taken care of. There was plenty of money to be made from government contracts for the grain shipments, and it was tax-free. In many places special seats were reserved in the theater for ship owners, a privilege designed to be a public mark of high status. We know that in many places

---

[1] Lampe, *From Paul to Valentinus*, 241.

[2] Judith M. Lieu, *Marcion and the Making of a Heretic: God and Scripture in the Second Century* (New York: Cambridge University Press, 2017), 50, 317.

[3] Lampe, *From Paul to Valentinus*, 256.

ship owners were the richest men in town, and they left many records of lavish donations and bequests.[4]

Marcion had traveled quite a bit, but by the time he entered history, he was a big enough man in the business that he didn't have to captain his own ships. He had people for that. He had become the CEO of a major concern, and that gave him leisure to read and write and think about things.[5]

By the time he moved to Rome, Marcion was already a Christian and already used to being a leader in the Church. He made a big splash in Rome, donating 200,000 sesterces to the Church there. That was a big deal. With a fortune of only half that amount, you were eligible to enter the lower rank of the Roman nobility, the decurions. With 400,000 sesterces to your name, you could be an equestrian, a very noble rank. Those 200,000 sesterces would have bought a nice estate in the country. You could get a hundred very good slaves for that money, and probably more than two hundred run-down slaves.[6]

With all his riches, Marcion lived very simply. He at least seemed not to care for worldly goods, though that didn't stop him from accumulating them. For a while he must have been a star in the Roman Church.

But in 144, he invited the priests and teachers of the Roman Church to a debate about the parables of the wineskins and the patched garment (see Luke 5:36–39). Here, apparently, the Christian leaders of Rome heard Marcion's peculiar ideas for the first time. The result was that they threw him out of the

---

4   Lampe, *From Paul to Valentinus*, 241–43.
5   Lampe, *From Paul to Valentinus*, 244.
6   See: Lieu, *Marcion and the Making of a Heretic*, 57; Lampe, *From Paul to Valentinus*, 245; Beacham, *Spectacle Entertainments*, 250n26.

Church—and gave him back his 200,000 sesterces.[7] (The dates are uncertain; another ancient source puts Marcion's break with the Catholic Church in 138.[8])

Marcion didn't let that stop him. If the Church wouldn't see things his way, the Church must be wrong. Marcion founded his own church—and he had money to back it up. In less than ten years, there were Marcionites in every province. Doubtless Marcion's extensive shipping interests helped in spreading his eccentric ideas. Many modern historians conclude that Marcion must have had a lot of organizational skills—the sort of skill you might expect from a successful shipping magnate.[9]

For an outsider, it was hard to tell a Marcionite church from a Catholic one, as St. Cyril of Jerusalem would later complain. The liturgy was very similar, in the same way that Lutheran, Anglican, and Catholic liturgies all seem similar today. But what Marcionites believed was very different from what any mainstream Christian group believes today.

WHAT MARCION TAUGHT

Marcion had picked up the Gnostic idea that creation was evil, the work of a lesser god. His teacher, says St. Irenaeus, was Cerdo, a follower of—guess who!—Simon Magus.

But Marcion had his own unique and radically simple version of that original Gnostic idea.

The God who created the world (Marcion said) is *just* but not *good.* He made evil, commanded cruel wars, and contra-

---

[7] Lampe, *From Paul to Valentinus*, 393.

[8] Lieu, *Marcion and the Making of a Heretic*, 296.

[9] See: Lampe, *From Paul to Valentinus*, 150; Lieu, *Marcion and the Making of a Heretic*, 396.

dicted himself in his teachings. This is the God of the law and the prophets—the God of Israel.

But there is another God—an unknown God—who is *good* and judges no one, but saves all equally. This nameless Stranger God sent Jesus Christ, who was a spirit in an illusion of a body, "like magic mist" with no real flesh.

There is no resurrection of the body, because the body is from the earth, created by the lesser God. Jesus came to rescue us from everything created by the God of the Old Testament, including our bodies.

And, of course, salvation is only for those who follow Marcion. Those who believe in the God of the Jews will be condemned—not because the good God, the Stranger God revealed for the first time by Marcion's Jesus, refuses to save them, but because they refuse to be saved.[10]

In fact, Marcionites had a very surprising story about that. They said

> that Cain and those like him, and the Sodomites, and the Egyptians, and in general all the nations that practiced all kinds of abominations, were saved by the Lord when he went down into Hades and they ran to him, and that he took them into his kingdom. But the serpent that was in Marcion declared that Abel, Enoch, Noah, and the patriarchs of the line of Abraham, along with all the prophets and those who were pleasing to God, did not share in salvation. For these people (he says) knew that their God was always testing them, so

---

[10] See Irenaeus, *Against Heresies* 1.27. See also *Five Books in Reply to Marcion* 93–119.

they suspected that he was testing them now, and did not run to Jesus or believe his announcement. And for this reason, he declared, their souls stayed in Hades.[11]

The Marcionites used the Old Testament, in the most clumsily literal reading, to argue that the Creator God, or "Cosmocrator" (the ruler of the world), was a lesser being and not good. "If the Creator is one and knew that Adam would sin against him," they asked, "why then did the Creator create?"[12] The good and perfect Stranger God had nothing to do with created matter.

Marcion took many of Jesus' parables and sayings as referring to the difference between his Father, the Stranger, and the God of the Jews. The patched garment and the wineskins, as we already saw, were two of the most important for him (Luke 5:36–39). No one puts a new patch on an old garment, and no one puts new wine in old wineskins. (New wine is still fermenting and the pressure would rip open the old wineskin.) That means, said Marcion, that we can't try to fit Jesus' teachings into the scheme of the Old Testament and its God. Marcion took the example of the armed man defeated by a stronger man (Luke 11:21–22) as referring to the Stranger God's defeat of the God of the Jews. "The Just One is mighty, but the Good One is mightier than he is." That's a Marcionite saying quoted by St. Ephrem.[13] When Jesus said that no one could serve two masters, Marcion explained, "mammon" referred to the God of the Jews (Luke 16:13).[14]

---

[11] Irenaeus, *Against Heresies* 1.27.3.
[12] See Lieu, *Marcion and the Making of a Heretic*, 68.
[13] Lieu, *Marcion and the Making of a Heretic*, 233.
[14] Lieu, *Marcion and the Making of a Heretic*, 233.

So for the Marcionites, redemption meant rescue from the power of the Creator, and thus from matter itself: the Stranger was foreign to both the Creator and his creation. The Latin theologian Tertullian got very sarcastic about this aspect of Marcion's teaching:

> Listen, you sinners! You who have not yet reached it, hear, that you may achieve sinfulness! A better god has been discovered, who never takes offense, is never angry, never punishes anyone, who has prepared no fire in hell, no gnashing of teeth in the outer darkness! He is purely and simply good. Yes, he forbids bad things, but that's just talk. He is in you, if you are willing to bow down to him—just for the sake of appearances, so that you may seem to be honoring God, for he doesn't want your fear.
>
> And the Marcionites are so satisfied with this make-believe that they have no fear of their God at all. They say only an evil being wants to be feared. A good one wants to be loved.[15]

Marcion based his ideas on some isolated pieces of Luke's Gospel, which was the only Gospel he recognized. But what about the large sections of Luke that obviously contradict Marcion? What about the parts that tell how Jesus was born of Mary, how he fulfilled the Old Testament prophecies, how his god is the God of Abraham, Isaac, and Jacob?

Here, Marcion had to resort to what modern scholars would call text criticism.

---

[15] Tertullian, *Against Marcion* 1.27.

Marcion's Scriptures

Armed with his new understanding of what Jesus really *meant*, Marcion was able to go back and edit Luke and the letters of Paul. The principle was simple. Whatever agreed with Marcion was obviously original. Whatever disagreed with him—whatever suggested that Jesus had been sent by the God of the Jews, the God of the Old Testament, the Creator—must have been added by ignorant Jewish-influenced editors. So Marcion took those latter passages out. And the whole Nativity narrative had to go, because Marcion's God would not have come to us through the messy material process of human birth.

Marcion, therefore, accepted one Gospel, heavily edited, and what Marcionites called the *Apostolicon*, which was an edited collection of ten of Paul's letters.

This editing set Marcion apart from other heretics in the eyes of his Catholic critics. Other heretics might add books to Scripture, but "he alone has openly dared to mutilate Scriptures," fumed Irenaeus. "Marcion and his followers are committed to cutting up the Scriptures—and, in fact, they do not accept all of them. Instead, they mutilate the Gospel according to Luke and the letters of Paul, and they claim that the only legitimate ones are the ones they have shortened themselves."[16]

Marcion didn't accept, by the way, that his Gospel was by Luke; he thought the title had been corrupted as well.

Without the Christmas story, Marcion's Gospel began with Christ's sudden appearance at Capernaum. He used the temporal setting of Luke 3:1, and then jumped to 4:31, inter-

---

[16] Irenaeus, *Against Heresies* 3.12.12.

preting "went down ['descended'] to Capernaum" to mean that he descended from heaven there.[17]

Aside from the nativity narratives, Marcion found many other parts of Luke that had to be deleted. He took out the parable of the fruitless fig tree in the vineyard (Luke 13:6–9) because it suggested judgment, and Marcion's God did not judge. He took out the parable of the wicked tenants (Luke 20:9–18) because it suggested that the God of the Jews was the one who sent Jesus. He took out the parable of the Prodigal Son (Luke 15:11–32) because it suggested that we needed to come *back* to the Father, and Marcion's God was a Stranger, hitherto unknown.

Marcion presented his alterations of Luke and Paul's letters as freeing them from Judaizing interpolations. Our canonical Luke "had been added to by the defenders of Judaism in order to *concorporate* the law and the prophets," as Tertullian explains Marcion's positions.[18] "To concorporate" (*ad concorporationem*) is a unique word, and although Tertullian was a great coiner of odd words, this one might have come straight from Marcion to describe the corruption he thought he found in the Catholic Christian Scriptures. Marcion thought his clever text criticism had detected these interpolations, but he was not a trained critic by modern standards—or by ancient standards. There were well-established methods of text criticism in Marcion's time, and by those standards, as well as ours, Marcion's work was sloppy and inconsistent.

Since Marcion's Jesus was not really human, it followed that he did not really die on the Cross. Marcion's account of the

---

[17] Lieu, *Marcion and the Making of a Heretic*, 214.

[18] Tertullian, *Against Marcion* 5.3.

Crucifixion left out the mockery and beating. Everything Jesus did in his apparent human form was only an illusion: "he ate and did not eat, drank and did not drink."[19]

But if the Son of God did not really die on the Cross, what was the point of the Passion? For Marcionites, it seems that Jesus ransomed us from sin and death by paying a literal ransom to the Creator for our souls (but not, of course, for our bodies).

ANTITHESES

Since Marcion's God did not judge, you might suppose that Marcionites could do anything they liked. But one of the things that most puzzled Marcion's critics was that he was positively puritanical. Marcion prohibited marriage, apparently because it created more slaves of the Creator God, prisoners in human bodies. He made continence a condition of baptism.[20] At least one source claims that Marcionites were vegetarian.[21] And we know there were Marcionite martyrs: the Marcionites might not be judged, but they were willing to die for Jesus.

Now, most of this teaching is clearly not what the tradition of the Church had handed down from the not-very-distant past. It was only eighty years after the death of Peter, the first leader of the Roman Church, that Marcion started his own church—and Peter certainly hadn't taught what Marcion was teaching. But Marcion had an answer for that: Peter was a false apostle.

---

[19] Reported by St. Ephrem in his *Hymns Against Heresies* 36.13, quoted in Lieu, *Marcion and the Making of a Heretic*, 172.

[20] Lieu, *Marcion and the Making of a Heretic*, 84, 130–31.

[21] Lieu, *Marcion and the Making of a Heretic*, 91.

In fact, the only reliable apostle, in Marcion's view, was Paul. Paul's rebuke of Peter in Galatians 2:11–21 was a key text for Marcion. And of course other parts of Paul's letters that showed Paul accepting Peter as a true apostle have been added by Judaizing Catholics. In the same way, Marcion took out all of Paul's references to Old Testament examples of faith because the Paul that Marcion imagined wouldn't have used them.

In addition to his one Gospel and the *Apostolicon*, Marcion or his followers composed a collection of psalms that Catholic churches had to warn their members against using, meaning that it must have been popular.

But Marcion's most famous work was his *Antitheses*, in which he pointed out what he thought were contrasts between the Old Testament God and his Stranger God.[22] The idea was to show that the God of the Jews and the God of Jesus could not be the same God. Tertullian called the *Antitheses* the Marcionites' chief document, "the one that introduced them to Marcion's ideas."[23] It might have served as a Marcionite catechism.[24]

In the *Antitheses*, Marcion tried to show that the God of the Jews was cruel and arbitrary, whereas the God of Jesus was good and nice. For example, he pointed out that (in his usual clumsily literal reading) David attacked the blind and lame, but Jesus healed them (2 Samuel 5:6–9; Luke 18:35–43). The children who mocked Elisha were eaten by bears, but Jesus loved little children and wanted us all to be like them (2 Kings 2:23–24; Luke 9:47–48).

---

22 Lampe, *From Paul to Valentinus*, 253.
23 Tertullian, *Against Marcion* 1.19.4.
24 Lieu, *Marcion and the Making of a Heretic*, 284.

FIGHTING BACK AGAINST MARCION

"I say my Gospel is true, Marcion his; I affirm Marcion's is corrupted, Marcion mine."[25] Tertullian realized that the battle against Marcion would have to be fought by proving that the Scripture Catholics accepted was the real Scripture, and that Marcion's alterations were false. Only thus could Tertullian argue that the God of the Old Testament was truly the same as the God of the New Testament. And this was the line of argument all the Catholic writers against Marcion used.

Tertullian, for example, argued that, because Marcion was the one making changes, the Gospel he was changing must be the original. Marcion, who thought the God of the Jews was the source of all evil, was making the same error as the Jewish writers: both denied that the Old Testament prophesied and typified Christ.[26]

But what *was* the place of the Old Testament in Christianity? Marcion's unwitting contribution to Catholic thought was forcing the Church to answer that question clearly.

In the Christianity passed down from the Apostles, the idea that the Old Testament foretold the coming of Christ was fundamental. Most early Christian art shows Old Testament scenes that Christians interpreted as foreshadowing the coming of Christ. The fulfillment of the prophecies was the favorite argument of Christian apologists even when they were talking to pagans.

But Christians are not bound by the law of the Old Testament, as Paul said: "But now we are discharged from the law,

---

[25] Tertullian, *Against Marcion* 29.9.
[26] Lieu, *Marcion and the Making of a Heretic*, 58–59.

dead to that which held us captive, so that we serve not under the old written code but in the new life of the Spirit" (Romans 7:6). In that way, at least, we agree with Marcion.

But the law was not proclaimed by an inferior God. Paul himself tells us (though Marcion probably took it out) that "the law is holy, and the commandment is holy and just and good" (Romans 7:12). But it was not meant to be a permanent arrangement: "the law was our custodian until Christ came" (Galatians 3:24).

St. Ephrem the Syrian explained that the law was like a sculptor's mold: the sculpture can't be made without it, but once the sculpture is cast, the mold passes away.[27] For Ephrem, the important point was that the two testaments speak of the same God, who behaves in the same way. This God is the Creator of the universe, and we can know him through nature as well as through Scripture. If nature is not good, why did Jesus heal people by returning them to their natural state? If Jesus came to undo the work of the Creator, he was doing a poor job of it.[28] In fact, total interdependence of body and soul is essential to Christian understanding. God made us as material beings; he will save us body and soul.

We can tell that Christ was from the God of the Old Testament, Catholic writers said, because he matches the types in and prophecies of the Old Testament. Therefore, said Tertullian, he must be "the Creator's Christ." A long verse treatise, *Five Books in Reply to Marcion*, insists that the Old Testament types show us that the same God came to us in Jesus:

---

[27] Ephrem, *Hymns Against Heresies* 36.8, quoted in Lieu, *Marcion and the Making of a Heretic*, 169.

[28] See Lieu, *Marcion and the Making of a Heretic*, 166–67.

See what virtue, see
What power the paschal image has: ye then
Will able be to see what power there is
In the true Passover.[29]

THE LEGACY OF MARCION

In the Simon Magus tradition, we saw evidence of a small anti-Paul faction in early Christianity. Marcion is the flip side: a pro-Paul extremist—one who would have made Paul himself blush.

The movement Marcion founded survived in various forms for centuries, gradually splitting and dwindling away. The Marcionites broke into factions based on (among other things) how many divine principles they admitted: Creator and Stranger; Creator, Stranger, and Devil; Creator, Stranger, and Matter; or just the Stranger, the Creator being an angel, not a god.

St. Cyril of Jerusalem was still talking about Marcionite parishes in his city two centuries after Marcion himself had disappeared from history. Epiphanius says that Marcionism was flourishing in Syria in his own time, the 300s. Archaeologists have found the remains of a "Synagogue of Marcionists," as an inscription at the site calls it, that was dedicated in the year 318. In the 400s, Theodoret of Cyrus claimed to have converted eight villages full of Marcionites. Even early Islamic writers were still refuting Marcionists.[30] It seems that Marcionism held on longer in the East.

Even there, the Marcionite sects eventually faded away. But

---

[29] *Five Books in Reply to Marcion* 2.88–91.
[30] Lieu, *Marcion and the Making of a Heretic*, 143, 179.

Marcion's anti-Jewish "Old Testament God vs. New Testament God" motif has haunted Christianity ever since.

The nineteenth-century scholar Adolf Harnack was the apostle of modern Marcionism. He thought that Marcion had figured out the really revolutionary implications of Christianity: "Marcion was the only Gentile Christian who understood Paul, and even he misunderstood him."[31] In other words, the only one smarter than Marcion was Harnack himself.

But the most notorious resurgence of Marcion's ideas was in Nazi Germany, where the Nazis—no Christians themselves—promoted a New-Testament-only Christianity for the masses. The idea, of course, was to purge Germans' Christian faith of anything that might create sympathy for the Jews. The Catholic Church rejected the Nazified Marcionism, of course, but many German Lutheran leaders fell for it. (To their eternal credit, some others, like Dietrich Bonhoeffer, preferred death.)

The Nazi experience points out the worst aspect of Marcionism. It starts out sounding like it's all about goodness and niceness—but it always seems to end with "and we really hate the Jews."

And when it reaches that point, goodness and niceness go out the window.

THE END OF MARCION

We don't really know what happened to Marcion in the end. There just isn't enough hard information about him. But Tertullian, writing not more than four decades after Marcion dies,

---

[31] Adolph Harnack, *History of Dogma*, vol. 1 (Boston: Little Brown, 1901), 89.

tells us that Marcion repented at last and the Church agreed to take him back if he would bring his followers back with him. But he died before he could manage it.[32] Once again, Christians imagine their longtime enemy repenting, but it's too late—a lesson to us all that we must not put off repentance.

The tale is probably too perfect to be true. But for the end of Marcion, it's all we've got.

---

[32] Tertullian, *Perscription Against Heretics* 30.

VALENTINUS

"For many deceivers have gone out in the world, men who will not acknowledge the coming of Jesus Christ in the flesh; such a one is the deceiver and the antichrist."

— 2 John 1:7

ALREADY BY THE time 2 John was written there were false teachers spreading an early form of Gnosticism. They said that God had not really come in human flesh, that Jesus Christ had only seemed to be human but was really a different order of being, or that the man Jesus was human, but the divinity had "come on" him when he was baptized by John and had left just before he was crucified. These ideas scandalized the Christians— some of the people who had known Jesus in the flesh were still alive. But the false teachers dismissed them as simple people. There was a secret wisdom Jesus taught only to a few, they said. *You aren't smart enough, so he didn't give it to you. But we're quite brainy, so he told us all about it.*

In other words, the most important parts of Gnostic teaching were already in place:

1. There is a secret teaching only for the few.
2. The Incarnation did not mean that God took on messy human flesh in a real way, because matter is evil.
3. We're a lot smarter than you.

According to legend, Simon Magus was the first Christian Gnostic, although Gnosticism really predates Christianity. There were pagan Gnostics and Jewish Gnostics. The idea of a secret wisdom that only a few of us are smart enough to understand has always been powerfully attractive. When Christianity came along the idea quickly adapted itself to the new faith.

There were as many variants of this Gnostic idea as there were Gnostic teachers, and there were probably as many Gnostic teachers as there were people who thought they were smarter than everybody else. But the one Gnostic group that seems to have worried the early Christians most—the one group they spent the majority of their time and effort refuting—was the Valentinians. They took their name from Valentinus, a Gnostic Christian who was very successful in Rome. And they worried the Catholics because, unlike most of the other heretics they had to deal with, the Valentinians were parasites on the Great Church.

VALENTINUS AND HIS SMART SET

We know almost nothing about Valentinus the man except that he was well educated. He had much more higher education than the average Christian: he had studied at Alexandria, so he had the ancient equivalent of a Harvard or Oxford degree. He had specialized in Platonic studies, meaning that he knew Plato backwards and forwards, at least as Plato was interpreted by later students who claimed to have understood him. (Like many philosophy students today, Valentinus probably learned about Plato from secondary sources more than from actually reading Plato.)

In about 130, Valentinus came to Rome and he stayed there for about twenty years. Thus, he was in Rome at the same time as Marcion. Valentinus later ended up in Cyprus.[1]

Of course, almost all the information we have about Valentinus' motivations comes from his opponents, so we have to allow for a little bias. Tertullian, who wrote a book titled *Against the Valentinians*, says that Valentinus had expected to be named a bishop in the Church, and walked out when he was passed over for somebody with fewer intellectual attainments but a more obviously Christian life. Thus, Tertullian derives Valentinus' whole project from jealous rage. Certainly people have nursed lifelong grudges for pettier causes.[2]

One thing his opponents gave Valentinus credit for was his brain. Tertullian and, much later, Jerome both considered him to have a formidable mind. But he applied that mind to creating an incredibly convoluted mythology rather than simply understanding the Scriptures. In this Valentinus was just like all the other Gnostics: incredibly convoluted mythologies were their stock in trade. The simple truth was for simple people. Like some academics today, the Gnostic teachers felt a need to prove

---

[1] Lampe, *From Paul to Valentinus*, 294–95.
[2] Tertullian, *Against the Valentinians* 4.

their intellectual worth by filling their writings with jargon nobody but other Gnostics could understand.

Boring from Within

The thing that worried the Catholic Church most, however, was not the intellectual capacity of the Valentinians. It was the way they deviously attached themselves to the Great Church and gradually sucked out some of the best and brightest members. Tertullian, who hated the Valentinians, grudgingly admired their skill in making converts. They built on standard Christian teaching at first, and only gradually revealed that there was a secret, much more elevated wisdom that you could learn about if you were patient and proved yourself worthy, possibly by making a substantial payment to your teacher.

Not by accident did the Valentinians target the rich among the Christians. The rich had money to pay for novel doctrines. Peter Lampe, a historian, marshals impressive evidence that, unlike the main body of the Church, most of the Valentinians in Rome lived in the best neighborhoods and had higher-level educations—and, above all, money.

And it was the rich among the Christians, not among the pagans or Jews, that the Valentinians targeted. Valentinians believed that the orthodox Church was the only possible preparation for the true Gnostic. In the ancient sources it is assumed that someone is first a "normal" Christian and only later evolves into a Valentinian Gnostic. Tertullian says that the Valentinians target "not the Gentiles, but our own."[3]

From their own point of view, the Valentinians were the

---

[3] Tertullian, *Prescription Against Heretics* 42.1.

inner, perfect core of the Church. It was the same Church; it was just that the orthodox Christians were not fully developed Christians. Most of them never would be. Valentinians saw a three-part hierarchy in the world: matter, soul, and spirit. Matter was evil and irredeemable. Most Christians were soul-Christians. But the Valentinians were spiritual beings.

Because they kept their secret doctrines to themselves, for a long time the Valentinians were accepted as fellow Christians by the Catholic Church in Rome. They were perfectly happy to live parasitically within the Church. Only when they identified a potential convert would they begin to hint subtly that if he (or she—there were many women among their converts) would care to delve deeper into the mysteries, there was someone willing to divulge these for a price.

DELIRIOUS MELONS

And what were those mysteries? Nothing less than the secrets of creation itself. In the simpleminded Scriptures for the ordinary Christian, God spoke and the world was created. But from the Valentinians you could learn what really happened.

In the beginning were the Primal Father and the feminine principle Thought, which had some sort of incomprehensible relations and produced Mind and Truth. Mind produced the Word, and the story goes on from there until thirty "aeons" have been produced in various ways. The last of the aeons was Wisdom, who made a fool of herself and tried to reproduce without a male principle, which naturally made her production worthless. This worthless production was Matter.[4]

---

[4] See Irenaeus, *Against Heresies* 1.1.

Jesus was produced by all the aeons working together. He was so perfect, the Valentinians said, that he ate without having to visit the restroom.[5]

This is a gross oversimplification of the Valentinian mythology, because none of us would have patience for the full version. And the full version kept changing anyway. Each Valentinian teacher freestyled his own version of the doctrine, and it didn't seem to matter that they disagreed.

One principle that followed from the teaching that Valentinians were spiritual beings was that their behavior—what they did with their material bodies—didn't really matter. So they did anything they liked. Spirit can't be destroyed; they were assured of salvation. Their material bodies were only prisons of the spirit that would pass away.

It was the great theologian St. Irenaeus who finally alerted the church in Rome to the danger of the Valentinians. And he did it by exposing their doctrines for everyone to see. Once they were out in the open, exposed without the careful preparation the Valentinians gave their converts, anyone could see how silly the Valentinian myths were.

But just in case the message didn't come through loud and clear, Irenaeus pounded the point home with a devastating bit of satire. First he describes the systems of aeons and emanations of some of the Valentinian teachers. And then he goes on from there:

> Alas, alack, and woe is me! For I may well use expressions
> from tragedy when he shows such daring—inventing

---

[5] See: Irenaeus, *Against Heresies* 1.4; Clement of Alexandria, *Stromateis* 3.7.59.3.

names shamelessly, making up a whole terminology for his system of lies. . . . Clearly he is the only one who was daring enough to invent these names. If he hadn't come along, the truth would have been nameless.

But in that case there's nothing to stop anyone else who talks about the same things from giving them names this way:

There is a certain Pre-Beginning, royal, beyond all thought, a power that exists before every other being and fills space in every direction. But along with it is a power which I denominate a Pumpkin, and along with this Pumpkin is another power which I denominate Nothing-at-All. This Pumpkin and Nothing-at-All, since they are one, produced, but did not merely produce so that it was different from them, a fruit which is everywhere visible, edible, and delicious, which in the language of fruits is called a Cucumber. With this Cucumber is another fruit of the same being, which I call a Melon. These powers—the Pumpkin, Nothing-at-All, the Cucumber, and the Melon—brought forth all the rest of the many delirious melons of Valentinus.

It didn't take long after Irenaeus' attack for the whole Church to realize that there was a parasite in their midst. From then on the Valentinians, once discovered, were routinely kicked out of the Catholic Church.

But Gnosticism of one form or another is amazingly persistent. It has been very fashionable in academic circles lately to bemoan the loss of "alternative" Christianities like Valentinianism. But they're never really lost. The idea that there is a hidden teaching not found in the Great Church is still a dogma among many sects that call themselves Christian. Large numbers of American Protestants believe the Valentinian doctrine of assured salvation for us, the few. We can laugh at the language of aeons and emanations and melons, but meanwhile, the worst parts of Valentinian doctrine may be sneaking up behind us.

CELSUS

THE EARLIEST CHRISTIANS had to deal mostly with Jewish arguments against what they believed. Pagans dismissed them as crazy cultists, if they even noticed Christians at all. But by the year 150 or so, everyone had heard of the Christians. They were still crazy cultists to most people, but there was a general impression of what they believed. They were atheists—because they refused to worship the gods known by everyone. They had secret rituals where they probably practiced cannibalism, because that's the sort of thing people like that would do. They formed secret societies where they planned their baby-eating atrocities. And if they were caught, they would go to their executions with a fanatical display of indifference, as if they actually believed in this resurrection they were always talking about.

In other words, most pagans in the Roman Empire of the first two centuries had a wildly mixed-up idea of what Christians believed, based on gossip and rumor. But there was one pagan writer who had actually bothered to find out what Christianity was all about. He did it for the sake of proving Christianity wrong and was mistaken in a lot of his assumptions about Christian belief. But give him credit: he tried. And because he was one of the most important scientific writers of the day, his work against the Christians was widely circulated and still referred to long after his death.

Celsus the Scientist

The man's name was Aulus Cornelius Celsus, and he was one of those remarkable people who seem to know a little bit about everything. Today we remember him most as a physician, because the main work of his that survives is a treatise on medicine; but that book was actually part of a book on practically all the world knowledge that Celsus had put together. He dealt with law, war, politics, farming, and other subjects as well. And if he knew as much about them as he did about medicine, Celsus must have been a one-man Wikipedia.

The medical treatise is really amazing from the point of view of the twenty-first century. Celsus describes delicate surgeries like facial reconstruction (using skin grafts!) and he knows the idea of antiseptics—an idea that eluded most American and European surgeons as late as a century and a half ago. If you had a serious problem that needed surgery, you would have been in good hands with Celsus.

The fact that Celsus was so insatiably curious about so many things may be why he bothered to try to learn about the Christians. They were a phenomenon to be studied. But his studies did not go so far as to ask the best authorities on the subject—the bishops and teachers he might have found if he had looked around. Instead, he seems to have relied on what he heard secondhand. That was probably because, although he was a scientist, Celsus was, like any good educated man in the Roman Empire, a snob first and foremost.

What's Wrong with the Christians?

What Celsus saw in Christianity was a combination of bad philosophy and stubborn fanaticism, but worst of all, lower-class prejudice. Nevertheless, he seems to have thought it was worth his while to argue with the Christians, and that suggests that he saw their numbers increasing. Christians were a danger because they preyed on unsuspecting people looking for the way to live the good life, and Celsus had to show why they were wrong.

First, he said, Christians call themselves monotheists, but obviously they're not. They make another divinity out of this Jesus, a criminal who started the whole sect. If God is God and Jesus is God, then there are two Gods, right? It almost seems that Christians can't count. Belief in one God might be excusable and even noble—Plato had come to the same conclusion. But believing in two Gods and calling them one is just confusion.

This Jesus was a charlatan who had succeeded in duping the gullible in Judea, but Celsus could see through his stories. Jesus obviously made up the story of the virgin birth. His mother really had an affair with a Roman soldier named Panthera (which was a common name for a soldier—sort of like "G. I. Joe" for Romans), and his father the carpenter threw her out of the house. As for the supposed miracles, obviously Jesus had learned magic when he was in Egypt. We've all seen the tricks of Egyptian magicians in the marketplace. Give them a few coins, and they'll show you all sorts of amazing illusions. Even rising from the dead was no big deal. Others have done it—plenty of characters in Greek mythology have gone down to the underworld and come back. And if you don't believe in their stories, why should we believe in yours? Besides, who saw this supposed resurrection? A few crazy women—*women!*—and maybe some other beggars who deluded themselves, or more likely wanted to impress people with an amazing story.

Here, by the way, we begin to see what really bothered Celsus about Christianity. It wasn't a religion for respectable people. It was lower-class.

No respectable God, for example, would actually come down to earth. Why couldn't an omnipotent God accomplish anything he wanted to get done from heaven? Do Christians really suppose that God got up and moved?

But what can we expect from people like these? Christians actually say that the wisdom of the world is evil, and foolishness is a good thing! (See 1 Corinthians 1:26–29.)

But it didn't take long for Celsus to come to what really bugged him about Christians. It wasn't so much the way they thought. It was that people like *those* presumed to think at all:

> And in private houses we see wool-workers, shoemakers, laundresses, and all kinds of illiterate hicks from the sticks. They wouldn't dare speak a word to people who are more respectable, or to their masters who actually have some learning. But when they're alone with the children and a few foolish women, they spew out the most appalling rubbish.[1]

---

[1]   Celsus, *On the True Doctrine.*

This is the thing that really gets to Celsus. Thinking is for respectable people, men of the upper classes who have the leisure for that sort of thing. That's why no upper-class Roman would presume to work with his hands. It simply isn't done. One has to have the leisure to develop one's mind. But these Christians are common workmen, slaves, even women—and yet they think they have the right to talk about things like God. They should just shut up and do what they're told. They should know their place.

In a way, Celsus, as a Roman, had the right instinct. It was impossible to take Christianity seriously without destroying the whole basis of the Roman class system. Christians really did believe that a shoemaker was as much a human being as a senator. That idea naturally filled an upper-class philosopher with horror. If that was true, what was the use of classes in the first place? Why would anyone go through all the trouble of being born rich?

But Celsus had also put his finger on what was making the Christian religion such a runaway success, in spite of the Empire's increasingly frantic attempts to squash it. In a world where most of the people would always be told they were worthless, the Christians bothered to say that God cared about *you* individually. He cared so much that he lived the life of a common workman—not a philosopher, not a senator, not even a decurion, but an ordinary carpenter. And there would come a time when the rich oppressor would understand that he had missed the boat—that he had been storing up treasure that would rust and be eaten by moths.

Ultimately, of course, Celsus would be found on the wrong side of history. His argument from class snobbery was the losing argument in a world where his class made up a tiny minority of the population. But his reputation as an encyclopedic philosopher meant that his work *Against the Christians* was still in circulation for quite some time after he died. Around a century or so after it was written, the book found its most able refutation in one of the greatest Christian writers of all time. And, by a curious quirk of history, that writer, Origen, also appears on our list of Christianity's early villains.

ORIGEN

OF ALL THE villains in the first few centuries of Christian thought, Origen is the strangest case. He's not really a villain at all. Yet he brought out some of the most venomous denouncements of the patristic era, as well as some of the most spirited defenses. In at least one case, the spirit and the venom came from the same famous writer at different times in his life.

The problem with Origen was that he was fantastically right about some things and fantastically wrong about others. But he was never a heretic, because he always submitted to the decision of the Church. It was his bad luck that he lived before the Church had made many of its most important decisions about theology, so he never got to submit to those decisions. But his speculations moved theology in the Christian world forward in a way that no amount of safe sticking to the tried and true would have done.

It's a complicated idea: to teach some of Origen's ideas today would be heresy, but Origen himself was not a heretic. It was too complicated for even some of the better Christian thinkers who came after him, and Origen's reputation suffered for it after his death. But today we can look back at him and see one of the great Fathers of the Church—and at the same time remember that we have to tread through his writings carefully. There are pits we can fall into if we're not careful.

Growing Up Christian

Origen was one of the relatively few among the early Christians who had the good luck to grow up Christian. He was born into a Christian family in about the year 185. It was a fairly comfortable Christian family, it seems, and Origen was sent to be educated in the usual Roman way.

Their typical method of education was pagan to the core. The whole curriculum was based on reading the ancient writers and learning good bits of them by heart. Since Origen lived in the East, he learned exclusively in Greek, and Homer, Plato, and the rest were his teachers. We know that even Christian children had to learn all the pagan mythology. One example of a young student's notebook has survived from ancient times by a bizarre fluke of preservation. In it we can see how the Christian boy copied out the lines from pagan authors, but added a Christian Chi-Rho monogram beside each quotation to neutralize the pagan content.[1]

Origen's father, Leonidas, gave him Bible lessons at home, and even as a young child, Origen was extraordinarily enthusiastic about Scripture. The historian Eusebius tells us that he used to embarrass his father with hard Bible questions that Leonidas couldn't answer. His father told him he shouldn't try to learn

---

[1]   See Lampe, *From Paul to Valentinus*, 353.

what was too much for him at that age, but of course he was secretly very proud of his boy.[2]

In the year 202, under Septimius Severus, one of the persecuting emperors, Leonidas was arrested. While he was imprisoned, his son sent him an encouraging letter begging him to go through with his martyrdom—which Leonidas did. Origen wanted to be martyred himself, but his mother hid his clothes so that the boy couldn't go out.

When Leonidas was executed his estate was confiscated, so Origen and his family—his mother and six brothers, all younger than Origen—were suddenly penniless. Thanks to a generous lady whose name has not come down to us, Origen was able to continue his studies, and he then supported his family by teaching grammar.

But that lasted for only about a year. At the age of eighteen, Origen was appointed a catechism teacher by his local church. The persecution was still hot; preparing for baptism was preparing for martyrdom. To throw himself completely into the work, Origen abandoned his paid teaching position and sold all his books of pagan literature. And at some point, he took a much more extreme measure: in order to be able to teach female catechumens without scandal or temptation, he castrated himself. (So Eusebius tells us[3]—and Eusebius was a great admirer of Origen. But some modern scholars think this was a slander circulated by Origen's enemies.)

This is a good example of Origen stepping over the line in his enthusiasm.

---

[2] Eusebius, *Church History* 6.2.
[3] Eusebius, *Church History* 6.8.

FAMOUS ALL OVER THE WORLD

It wasn't long before Origen's reputation began to spread through Alexandria, where he taught, and then from Alexandria into the rest of the Roman world. Origen's teaching was different. He was by all accounts a spellbinding speaker and he put his thorough education in the classics to good use. In fact, he began to study pagan philosophy much more thoroughly, plundering all the philosophers' best thoughts and putting them at the service of Christian education. "The fact that the law we follow was given to us by God does not entitle us to swell with pride and refuse to listen to the wise," he said. "No, as the Apostle says, we should 'test everything' and 'hold fast what is good'" (referencing 1 Thessalonians 5:21).[4]

What had started as a teaching position grew into a kind of Christian philosophical university. "Thousands of heretics and many of the most eminent philosophers eagerly flocked to hear him and were not ashamed even to pick up points about secular philosophy from him as well as to hear about Christian doctrine," Eusebius tells us. And a little later, "The Greeks themselves [a.k.a., pagans] admitted that he was a great philosopher."[5]

In a letter to one of his former students, Origen explained that every kind of knowledge was useful in the study of the Christian faith. "So I hope you'll take everything from Greek philosophy that can serve as an introduction to Christianity, and all the things from geometry and astronomy that will help expound the Holy Scriptures." Just as all these studies are com-

---

4   Gregory Thaumaturgus, *Oration and Panegyric Addressed to Origen* 15.
5   Eusebius, *Church History* 6.18.

monly said to be philosophy's assistants, we should be able to say that philosophy is Christianity's assistant.[6]

In learning philosophy, Origen told his students that they should try all the systems but not stick to just one of them. Instead, they should take whatever is worth taking from each one of them.

As he taught in Alexandria and then in Caesarea in Palestine, Origen's reputation spread throughout the empire—so much so that he was summoned by the pagan empress, who wanted to hear the great Christian philosopher everyone was talking about. The Roman upper classes were very eclectic in their religion, and even an emperor might well include Christ among the many gods to whom he addressed his prayers. Why not? Might as well cover all the bases. It wasn't worshipping Christ that made the Christians outlaws: it was their refusal to worship anyone else, including the genius of the emperor.

Origen's reputation was certainly helped by what quickly became a prodigious literary output. He may well have been the most prolific writer of ancient times. A rich patron named Ambrose financed a whole literary workshop for Origen. "At least seven shorthand reporters worked in shifts and transcribed his dictation," Eusebius tells us. "And there were the same number of copyists and girls who were professional engrossers."[7] Origen's works went straight from his mind into publication, copied as soon as they were transcribed by the large staff Ambrose provided for him.

But all this attention didn't make Origen's bishop very happy. Already Origen's flights of speculation were beginning

---

[6] Origen, *Letter to St. Gregory Thaumaturgus.*
[7] Eusebius, *Church History* 6.23.1.

to get him in trouble—as, for example, when he speculated that since the devil had fallen by his own free will, then it must be possible for him to repent. When Origen was ordained a priest in Palestine rather than in his own diocese, and in spite of his self-mutilation, both of which were quite irregular, he was expelled from the Church in Alexandria. But the excommunication wasn't recognized in Caesarea, which he made his new home. The writing factory that Ambrose had paid for, however, did not go with him. He lost some of what he had dictated in the move and had to start over again.[8]

So already we see in Origen's lifetime that his opinions could generate controversy. But he was not a stubborn man and he was always willing to give up an opinion if the Church decided definitively against it. In fact, Origen always described himself as a "man of the Church." He believed that Christ could be found only in the Church:

> We should not listen to those who say, "Look! Here is Christ!"—but do not point him out in the Church, which is full of his radiance from east to west, which is full of true light, which is the pillar and foundation of truth.[9]

He might speculate freely, but Origen's faith never wavered. It was so obvious to the people around him, in fact, that they gave him a nickname: Adamantius, the man with the diamond-hard faith.

Origen did finally get to fulfill his ambition to be a martyr. He was an old man by the time it happened, but at last, in the

---

[8] Origen, *Commentary on St. John's Gospel* 6.2.9–11.
[9] Origen, *Sermon on Matthew* 47.

persecution of Decius, he was arrested and tortured. He was not executed—his torturers probably wanted him to abide as a cautionary tale against the Christian faith—but he died shortly afterward, probably from his injuries.

His work lived on, however. It brought Christian theologians a new set of tools, more powerful than any they had had to work with before. It would also eventually bring bitter arguments and accusations of heresy.

ORIGEN'S LEGACY

Everything Origen taught was founded on the interpretation of Scripture. "His essential idea," wrote the twentieth-century scholar Jean Danielou, "may be said to be that the Logos is present under the accidents of the Scriptures as food for the soul."[10] Everywhere you look in Scripture, he thought, you find Christ. But you have to know how to look.

> We believe that the Scriptures were written by the Spirit of God and that in addition to their literal meaning they have another, which the majority of people are unaware of. The things written in the Scriptures are signs of certain mysteries and images of the things of God.[11]

In other words, Origen was a champion of what we call the typological interpretation of Scripture, in which we find images of the truths of Christian faith in the Old Testament as well as in the New. This is standard Christian doctrine, since

---

[10] Jean Danielou, *Origen* (Eugene, OR: Wipf and Stock, 2016 [1955]), 131.
[11] Origen, *De principiis* 1, praef. 8.

both Jesus and Paul saw many of the Old Testament stories as images of the truth of the Incarnation. But Origen made his whole system out of typological interpretation.

However, before he could proceed to a typological interpretation, Origen had to be sure of the literal interpretation. And that meant that he had to establish the correct text of Scripture. So, singlehandedly, Origen invented the science of biblical text criticism.

Origen went even further than this, though: St. Jerome reminds his readers that, "as everyone knows, he was so devoted to Scripture that he even learned Hebrew, which at that time nobody did in his country."[12] And learning Hebrew was only the beginning of Origen's work. "With the help of God's grace," Origen wrote, "I have tried to solve the problem of the variants in the different copies of the Old Testament by checking one version against another."[13] To do that, he compiled a text known as the Hexapla, because it laid six versions of the Old Testament side by side:

1. The Hebrew text,
2. A Greek transliteration of the Hebrew text,
3. The Septuagint translation,
4. Symmachus' Greek translation,
5. Aquila's Greek translation, and
6. Theodotion's Greek translation.

In the case of the Psalms, Origen had eight texts to work with, one of which he had found in an old barrel in Jericho.[14]

---

[12] Jerome, *Illustrious Men* 54.
[13] Origen, *Commentary on St. Matthew* 15.14.
[14] Eusebius, *Church History* 6.16.3.

Making a detailed study of Scripture like that, Origen was able to come to some surprisingly modern-sounding conclusions. For example, there was the long-standing question of who wrote the Epistle to the Hebrews. The book itself doesn't tell us, but it was often attributed to Paul. Origen, however, came to a different conclusion: "The style . . . lacks the simplicity characteristic of the Apostle's: St. Paul admits that he is rough in his speech, whereas the Epistle is typically Greek in the artistry of its style." These are the observations modern scholars make about the book, and most of them go on to reach the same conclusion Origen came to: "If I had to give an opinion, I should say that the thought was the Apostle's but that the phrasing and composition came from the person who wrote the Apostle's teaching down."[15]

The Old Testament in particular was a fertile ground of disagreement among Christians, as it still is today. To Origen, the fatal error in interpreting the Old Testament was almost always over-literalism. As St. Paul tells us, we have been freed from the burden of the law, so we need to understand how the Old Testament is relevant to us as Christians as well as what it originally meant to the ancient Hebrews. Origen picked out three errors in particular:

1. Over-literalism of the Jews, which led them to think that Jesus did not fulfill the prophecies.
2. Over-literalism of the Marcionites, which led them to suppose that the Old Testament God was a different God.
3. Over-literalism of many Christians in the Church, which leads them to think that God is cruel and vindictive.

---

[15] Quoted in Eusebius, *Church History* 6.25.12.

To avoid these errors, we need to interpret the Old Testament spiritually and we need to interpret it within the tradition of the Christian Church: "We insist that we can accept as the truth only what does not conflict with the tradition of the Church and of the Apostles in any way."[16]

St. Paul himself gives us a good example of an allegorical interpretation of the Old Testament in Galatians 4:21–31, when he tells us that Hagar and Sarah represent the two covenants. For Origen, this was a good example of how Christians should understand the Old Testament. Although it was important to understand the literal meaning of the Old Testament, Christians were no longer bound by that literal meaning. The New Testament is the reality for which the figures of the Old Testament prepared us. "The water of Merah kills if it is drunk without being changed," Origen said, himself adopting a metaphor from the Old Testament (see Exodus 15:22–25) to explain his principle of interpretation.

> And who is such a fool as to believe that God, acting like a farmer, "planted a garden in Eden, in the east," and in it put a "tree of life" that could be seen and touched . . . and that you could ingest good and evil by chewing and swallowing the fruit taken from the tree with that name? And when it says that God was "walking in the garden in the cool of the day," and that Adam hid behind a tree, I do not believe anyone will doubt that these are figurative expressions that signify certain mysteries by means of stories, not by actual events.[17]

---

[16] Origen, *De principiis* 1, praef. 2.
[17] Origen, *Homilies on Exodus* 7.

So far this is all orthodox Catholic thinking, and you'll find the same thoughts in many of the other Fathers of the Church. And Origen's conclusion is perfectly orthodox as well: "If you want to understand *these* things, you cannot—except through the Gospel."[18] We could say that it's the way Jesus himself taught us to read the Old Testament as all referring to him. "You search the scriptures, because you think that in them you have eternal life; and it is they that bear witness to me; yet you refuse to come to me that you may have life. . . . If you believed Moses, you would believe me, for he wrote of me. But if you do not believe his writings, how will you believe my words?" (John 5:39–40, 5:46–47). We are like blind people whose eyes need to be opened by Jesus before we can understand the Scriptures.

But although Origen believed in the importance of understanding the literal meaning of Scripture, there were many even while he was alive who thought that his spiritual interpretations went quite a bit too far.

GOING TOO FAR

Origen wrote something like a thousand works of various lengths, and in them he gave many interpretations of Old Testament stories—sometimes different interpretations of the same story. This was not a fault in Origen's view: for him, the same story could have many interpretations. The Exodus was an event in history, but it could also be the passage from error to truth or the passage from this world to the next. All three interpretations, and more besides, could be true at the same time.

---

[18] Origen, *Homilies on Genesis* 7.5.

So there's a certain improvisational quality to some of Origen's Old Testament interpretations, and even his New Testament interpretations. In the Gospels as well as the Old Testament, he sees allegories everywhere. Jesus was baptized on the fifth day of the fourth month: that refers to the four elements of the body and the five senses of the soul. Some Christians thought this sort of reading was going too far. Jesus could have been baptized on the fifth day of the fourth month because that was when John and Jesus happened to be in the same place at the same time. It doesn't have to mean anything else.

Origen also tended to speculate freely about things like the creation of the world and the end of it. We have to remember that, in his time, many theological questions had not yet been answered by the Church as a whole. When did the soul enter the body? What was there before the universe was created? "For it is a capital sin to understand the divine dogmas otherwise than as the Church holds," Origen wrote.[19] But where the Church didn't have an opinion, Origen felt free to make his own guesses.

So, for example, Origen seems to have a subordinationist view of the relationship of the Son to the Father, meaning that he puts the Son far below the Father in eminence. The later heretic Arius would take this idea and run with it, forcing the Church to define its doctrine that the Father and Son are of the same being. But the doctrine hadn't been defined yet in Origen's time. He was sailing in uncharted waters.

Origen speculated that souls must exist before the bodies. This, he reasoned, would explain why some are born blind or lame or with other difficulties: they had sinned in a previous existence. Before the world was created, all spirits had been

---

[19] Origen, *Homilies on Leviticus* 8.

made equal, he thought, but in their pre-embodiment existence they earned different levels of merit through their own free will. Thus, in the course of creation, some were born as stars, some as humans, and some as angels or demons. All spirits sinned, but angels and archangels sinned less, demons more, humans somewhere in the middle.

Origen also believed that the judgment on the demons was not final. In fact, he believed that all spirits would be saved eventually. There would be multiple creations of multiple worlds so that even the worst—even Satan himself—would eventually be brought back to God.[20]

In these and many other speculations Origen ended up going astray from what the Church would ultimately decide. But, again, we must remember that those decisions hadn't been made yet. And Origen always submitted his ideas to the judgment of the whole Church. "I bear the title of a priest," he wrote, "and, as you see, I preach the word of God. But if I do anything contrary to the discipline of the Church or the rule laid down in the Gospels—if I give offense to you and the Church—then I hope the whole Church will unite with one consent and cast me off."[21]

Origen dies having no idea how close the Church would come to doing just that.

The Case against Origen

The first charges against Origen were actually brought by pagan opponents. In fact, one of the bitterest denouncements came from a man who had known Origen when they were

---

[20] See: Danielou, *Origen*, 270; Origen, *De principiis* 1.6.3.
[21] Origen, *Homilies on Joshua* 7.6.

young students together: Porphyry, who became a well-known philosopher.

> Some people, who are trying to figure out how to get away from the poverty of the Hebrew writings without getting rid of them altogether, had recourse to commentaries that make no sense and have nothing to do with the words themselves. . . . They find puzzles in what Moses said clearly, and gravely announce that these are oracles filled with subtle mysteries. . . . This sort of foolishness comes from someone I met when I was very young: Origen.[22]

But there were also Christians who thought Origen's allegorical interpretations of Scripture had gone too far. They thought the literal sense was being lost in the torrent of supposed spiritual senses.

Against those critics, St. Jerome, one of the greatest minds of Christian history, defended Origen with his usual blunt vigor: "Origen, whom, as (after the Apostles) a teacher of the churches, no one would deny unless he was an idiot."[23] Jerome had a simple explanation for these criticisms of Origen: the great Adamantius was condemned "not for novel dogmas, not for heresy (as rabid dogs now pretend against him), but because they couldn't bear the glory of his eloquence and knowledge, and because when he spoke, all others were thought dumb."[24]

But later we find Jerome grumbling that Origen was "always an allegorical interpreter, and fleeing the truth of history." From

---

[22] Eusebius, *Church History* 6.19.

[23] Jerome, *On Hebrew Names* preface.

[24] Jerome, *Letters* 33 (to Paula).

Origen's biggest fan, he suddenly turned into Origen's mortal enemy. (Well not really mortal, since Origen had already been dead for about a century and a half.) His frequent correspondent St. Augustine, possibly the only greater mind in the Church at the time, noticed the change with some concern: "Indeed, I read that Origen and Didymus are reprehended by you in your more recent works, and that not lightly or in light matters, though before you had praised Origen marvelously."[25]

What happened?

Just before the year 400, Rufinus, a prolific Latin writer and translator, had produced a translation and adaptation of Origen's *De principiis*, or "On First Principles," as the title is usually translated. What followed was a sensational controversy in Rome, because *De principiis* included some of Origen's wildest speculations. At first, Jerome blamed Rufinus, and in fact it's hard to tell whether Jerome ever really blamed Origen for the controversy. It was certainly true that Rufinus had been very free in his translation. At any rate, the Origenist controversy eventually roiled the whole Christian world, even as far away as Bethlehem, where Jerome was living at the time. Jerome himself eventually identified eight false teachings that could be found in *De principiis* that had to be repudiated by Catholic Christians:

1. That the Son cannot see the Father, and the Spirit cannot see the Son.
2. The pre-existence of the soul.
3. The eventual salvation of the devil and the demons.
4. That Adam and Eve had no flesh before the fall.
5. The denial of the resurrection of the flesh.

---

[25] Augustine, *Letters* 82.3.23.

6. The over-allegorization of Paradise.
7. The interpretation of the waters above the heavens as holy essences, and waters above and beneath the earth as demonic essences.
8. That the "image of God" was lost in man after the Fall.[26]

The controversy raged hot enough that Pope Anastasius had to step in and make an official statement. It was a very careful condemnation: he didn't condemn Origen, but rather condemned "everything written by Origen in the past that contradicts our faith."[27]

Jerome's friend and former student Marcella was prominent among the anti-Origenist party in Rome, allying herself with her old teacher in his anti-Origen phase. Jerome describes the controversy as "a whirlwind of heresy." But even here he seems to accuse Rufinus more than Origen: he talks about "the scandalous translation of Origen's book" and describes it as "emended by the hand of the scorpion," as if Rufinus were to blame for whatever is heretical.[28]

Not everyone praised Jerome's response in this controversy. Palladius, who knew Jerome, thought his hot temper eclipsed all his laudable accomplishments, and he also praised Rufinus as a very learned and kind man. But it was the condemnation of Origen's *On First Principles* that was the lasting result of the fight.

In one of history's little jokes, it turns out that Rufinus' "emended" version of Origen's *On First Principles*—the translation that Jerome blamed for starting the whole controversy—is

---

[26] Jerome, *Letter to Pammachius Against John of Jerusalem.*
[27] Quoted in Jerome, *Letters* 95.2.
[28] Jerome, *Letters* 127.

all we have of the book. Origen's Greek original is lost, except for stray quotations in other writers' works.

That's because, about a century and a half later, the emperor Justinian was determined to root out all heresy from his territory. Justinian was not a well-educated man, but he was enthusiastic. He had heard that Origen's works were heretical, so he had them systematically rounded up and destroyed. We're lucky to have what we do have: a tiny fraction of the thousand books Origen wrote.

ORIGEN TODAY

So what do we make of Origen? Was he a heretic?

The Church today would give a more measured response to that question than Justinian gave. Origen was never a heretic, because he never deliberately taught anything contrary to the teachings of the Church. In fact, as we saw, he very specifically submitted his thought to the judgment of the whole Church and asked that anything incorrect be rooted out. Where he was wrong, he was venturing into areas that hadn't been defined by the Church yet. And where he was right, he advanced Christian theology further than anyone before him.

Perhaps we can let Origen himself have the last word in his own story, because he shows us how a Christian theologian can be daring and humble at the same time.

> I who call myself a man of God, I who receive the Holy
> Book and strive to interpret it, I ask those who hear
> me to pay close attention to see that I do not fall into
> the error of the heretics and to exercise, with the grace
> of the Holy Spirit, the discernment of spirits, in order

to observe, like clever moneychangers, when I am a master of error and when I am teaching according to piety and truth.[29]

---

[29] Origen, *Homilies on Ezekiel* 2.

DIOCLETIAN

IN THE 200s, the Roman Empire fell apart. For decades, disaster after disaster rolled across the Mediterranean world. Civil war was the normal state of political affairs. The economy fell to pieces. Plagues ravaged the cities and countryside. Emperors lasted for a few months and then were assassinated by their own guards, who knew that the next emperor would pay them a hefty bonus to get on their good side and that they could repeat the whole process again in a few months' time and get another hefty bonus.

And then came Diocletian, and suddenly the world worked again. He came very close to being remembered as one of history's greatest heroes, the man who saved civilization when it was on the brink of collapse.

Instead, he found himself backed into a corner he couldn't get out of, and the world of the future would remember him as a monster.

THE BIG PLAN

After he defeated all his rivals, Diocletian put together a plan that would save the Roman Empire from chaos and civil war for the rest of time. It was remarkably simple and very clever, and there was no way it could possibly fail.

Diocletian divided the empire into two halves, and then the two halves each into two halves. In each half-empire, the West and the East there would be a senior emperor and a junior emperor, each governing half the territory. After a certain time, the senior emperor, the Augustus, would retire, and the junior emperor, the Caesar, would become the Augustus. Then the new Augustus would pick the most able young man in his half of the empire to be his new Caesar. The process would continue forever.

It seemed reasonable that this plan should solve all the problems. Experience had shown that trouble could break out anywhere in the empire and one emperor might well be months of travel away from the crisis when it happened. But four emperors would be distributed around the empire so that one of them would always be fairly near to any trouble. And the young Caesars would know that they would become Augusti in time, so they would have no reason to assassinate the current incumbents. It was to their advantage that the transition should be as smooth as possible, so they wouldn't have any fires to put out when they reached the top spot.

But pure reason wasn't enough. People needed to *feel* that their emperors were in control. They needed faith in their government. And so Diocletian went back to the tried-and-true policy of mixing up Roman politics with Roman religion. He made himself the representative of old-fashioned Roman values.

And, like many who paint themselves as the voices of old-fashioned values, he ended up creating something entirely new in Roman politics.

STATE AND SUPERSTITION

From the beginning of Rome, of course, Roman government and Roman religion had been tightly linked. Rome was no different in that way from every other place on earth.

But the emperors tried to make sure that the Roman religion was linked not just with the state but with the emperor himself. Augustus, the founder of the empire, made sure that everyone knew that he was the destined ruler, put there by the gods to make Rome great. The greatest work of ancient Latin literature, the *Aeneid,* was sponsored by Augustus as a propaganda piece to tell the world that destiny had picked him out from the beginning of Roman history.

"What in other peoples is an object of reproach—I mean superstition—is the very thing that maintains the cohesion of the Roman State," wrote the historian Polybius. "These matters are clothed in such pomp and introduced to such an extent into their public and private life that nothing could exceed it. . . . Their object is to use it as a check upon the common people. . . . Since every multitude is fickle, full of lawless desires and violent passion, it must be kept in check by invisible terrors and suchlike pageantry."[1] Everything the government did was linked with Roman religion, and the emperor was the head of the Roman religion and its chief visible object. "Caesar and the republic have been combined for so long that they cannot

---

[1] Polybius, *Histories* 6.56

be pulled apart without destroying both." So wrote Seneca in Nero's time,[2] when the Romans were only just beginning to discover the strange new cult that refused to bow to Caesar's image.

What had always been the theory would become Diocletian's dogma, the pillar of his new and improved imperial system. The people of the empire would have to be impressed by their emperor. He would have to be visibly superior in every way. Actually, Diocletian was a rough-hewn old soldier, but he insisted on an elaborate court ceremonial, with gorgeous costumes and intricate choreography, that was all designed to present one message to anyone who saw it: something divine is in our midst.

The ceremony was impressive, and Diocletian and his fellow emperors in the four-emperor scheme managed to restore status and confidence. There was only one big problem. In spite of the impressive pageantry, the large and growing Christian population wasn't impressed.

THE ACCIDENTAL PERSECUTOR

Diocletian really had nothing against Christians. He was a superstitious pagan himself, but he had Christian friends. There were even Christians in his administration. For decades now, though the laws against Christians had not officially changed, no one had tried to persecute the Christians. They had prospered and multiplied, and there was a Christian church practically right next to Diocletian's palace. For the better part of two decades, Diocletian had left the Christians alone, just as his predecessors had done.

---

[2] Seneca, *On Mercy* 1.4.3.

But his Caesar Galerius had a mother who loathed the Christians. She was a superstitious devotee of the mountain gods, and she relentlessly poked at her son, demanding that he do something about the Christian infidels who defied the laws and refused to revere the gods.

Galerius took the matter to Diocletian, and to his credit, Diocletian resisted for a long time. *The Christians are doing no harm, he said, and there is no reason to fill the empire with blood. Besides, you know how those Christians are: they actually welcome martyrdom. Better to leave them be and just make a rule that no one in government can be a Christian.*

Galerius, however, was not willing to be reasonable about the Christians. So Diocletian decided to get some advice.

This was a bad sign.

Now, Diocletian's wicked disposition had this peculiarity: whenever he decided to do something good, he did it with no consultation, so that he could take all the credit for it, but whenever he decided to do something evil, he called in many to give advice, so they could take the blame for what he was going to do.[3]

The advisers were taken from both the civil government and the military, but Galerius let them know beforehand what opinion he expected them to give. There would be trouble if Diocletian didn't get the right advice. Many of them had nothing against Christians, but they all had a strong desire not to feel the wrath of Galerius, who was apparently a force to be

---

[3] Lactantius, *On the Deaths of the Persecutors* 11.

reckoned with, especially when he was doing what his mother told him to do.

Even so, Diocletian wasn't quite ready to take the unanimous advice he received. (It's possible he knew Galerius well enough to know why the advice was unanimous.) He decided to consult the gods. The gods also gave the answer Galerius wanted them to give, possibly because the answer came through a soothsayer who was easily influenced. Diocletian would have to deal with the Christians.

But what should he do about them? Burn them all alive if they refuse to sacrifice, said Galerius, a man of strong opinions. Diocletian, however, was not going to go that far. Surely this whole problem could be solved without bloodshed. The Christians would see reason when they saw that he was serious.

The persecution was let loose first on the big church that could easily be seen from Diocletian's palace in Nicomedia. Soldiers burst through the doors at dawn and demanded to know where the statue of the god was. Clearly they didn't understand much about Christianity; they were puzzled when they couldn't find the object of worship. They did find a Bible, however, and burned that, which made them feel better. Then they looted the church, which made them feel a lot better.

Galerius and Diocletian were watching from a tower in the palace, and the pyromaniac Galerius kept trying to have the church burned to the ground. But Diocletian wouldn't let him do that. "Are you crazy?" he said. "You'll set the whole city on fire!" They finally compromised and had the soldiers level the church with axes and demolition tools.[4]

---

[4] Lactantius, *On the Deaths of the Persecutors* 12.

THE GREAT PERSECUTION

That was the beginning, and it is doubtless that Diocletian hoped it would be nearly the end. Christians would understand that they had to follow the laws, which were really quite simple. Make a sacrifice of incense to the genius of the emperor and you've shown that you're a loyal Roman. What's so hard about that?

But of course that was exactly the sort of thing Christians wouldn't do.

Diocletian's first edict deprived the Christians of their civil rights: they could not hold office or vote in elections, and lawsuits would automatically be decided against them. Then there was an order to round up all the bishops and force them to sacrifice. And then the Scriptures would have to be turned in for destruction. And then, finally, every single person in designated cities would have to get a certificate documenting that he had made a sacrifice to the genius of the emperor.

Diocletian had tried to be reasonable. But once Galerius had manipulated him into starting the persecution, the persecution seemed to have a mind of its own. It got bigger and bloodier until it had the whole empire in an uproar. Where Diocletian had hoped to be remembered as the emperor who restored peace, he had become the emperor who instigated the bloodiest persecution the Mediterranean world had ever seen.

The scenes were repeated all over the empire: Diocletian's Gestapo kicks down the door and demands to know where the holy books are. Men, women, and children are taken off to prison to wait for their turn in front of the judge. And when they get there, they're given a simple choice: sacrifice now and go back home free, or refuse and die a horrible death. If they have trouble making the choice, there are many creative tortures to help them make up their minds. And all these proceedings are carefully recorded by court reporters, because if there was one thing the Romans were good at, it was bureaucracy. Some of those have survived to the present day, carefully copied—ironically enough—by the Christians.

There were many Christians who did make the choice to live now: they had grown up in the decades of peace and prosperity, and they had no experience of real persecution. But many more made the other choice. They were burned, or thrown to the beasts for the entertainment of the sadistic populace, or whatever else seemed as if it would send the right message. Yet, there were still Christians. For eight years, from 303 to 311, the persecution raged, and yet there was no collapse of the Christian Church, no fall in the numbers of Christians. If anything, the examples of the martyrs added to the number of Christians.

Diocletian himself retired in 305, as he had planned, and the orderly machine of succession he had so carefully constructed immediately stripped its gears. Soon there was a mad scramble of six different Augusti, each claiming to be the real Augustus and each trying to kill all the other Augusti. Civil war had returned to the empire and the persecution was still going on. Diocletian himself decided to come out of retirement and sort everything out. He was universally ignored, and he went home to his vast palace in what is now Croatia and killed himself.

The End of the Persecution

Yet, the persecution Diocletian had unwillingly set in motion still had years to go. Eventually, though, it became obvious that not even death would stop the Christians. It was—in one of history's splendid jokes—Galerius himself, the fanatical Christian-hater who had wanted to see them all burn, who actually issued the first edict tolerating Christianity. According to Christian writers, the superstitious Galerius had a Christian doctor who convinced him that the horrible disease he was suffering from was a punishment from the Christian God for persecuting his followers. Whatever his reason, he finally gave up in 311. He pointed out that his edicts had been successful in bringing many Christians back from their foolish superstition. "However, there were a great many who remained determined," he observed. "Therefore, taking into account our very merciful nature, and our invariable habit of pardoning everyone, we have decided that it is right to give them our immediate indulgence in this case as well, so that Christians may exist again, and may build their places of meeting, as long as they are not disorderly in any way."[5]

According to the Christian story, Galerius then died in agony, cursing the Christian God for not curing his disease after he had done him such a favor.

Galerius' edict was valid only in the territory he controlled. But meanwhile, in the West, the world was changing. A young would-be emperor named Constantine was about to move in on Rome itself, and on the eve of his great battle, he had a vision of a cross in the sky with the words "In this sign you shall conquer."[6]

And so when Constantine fought the climactic battle for Rome, he fought under the banner of the Cross. And he won. The world was changed forever. Diocletian and his persecution

---

[5] Lactantius, *On the Deaths of the Persecutors* 34.

[6] Sozomen, *Ecclesiastical History* 1.3.

were history. Christianity was made legal throughout the empire, and it was the preferred religion of the Western emperor himself.

But which kind of Christianity? Much to his surprise, Constantine discovered he was going to have to answer that question if he really wanted peace in his domain.

ARIUS

ARIUS WAS an obscure Egyptian priest who probably had more influence on the history of Christian theology than any Christian thinker since St. Paul. It was all negative influence, but no one can deny the influence. Because of Arius, the Catholic Church had to define the relationship of the Son to the Father in clear and unambiguous terms. Because of Arius, we ended up with the Nicene Creed.

But no one would have guessed for most of his life that this Arius was going to set the world on fire.

AN OBSCURE LIFE UNTIL . . .

Arius was probably born in Libya, and that word "probably" is going to come up again and again when we talk about his life. He was probably born in the 250s, but no one knows for sure. By about the year 310, he was a priest in Alexandria in Egypt. So for the first sixty years of his life, he did very little that history remembers.

He was very tall, with a downcast countenance—coun-
terfeited like a wily serpent, and quite able to fool the
unsuspecting with his artistically arranged appearance.
He always wore a short cloak and a sleeveless tunic; he
spoke quietly, and people found him persuasive and
flattering.[1]

This description was obviously written by somebody who
didn't like Arius very much. But Epiphanius does probably preserve a couple of useful details. Arius' quiet, persuasive voice
must have had something to do with the sudden notoriety
that came to him late in life. And the way he dressed was cal-
culated to make an impression. As the scholar (and Anglican
Archbishop of Canterbury) Rowan Williams explained, "Arius'
costume would have identified him easily as a teacher of the way
of salvation—a guru, we might almost say."[2] In other words,
everything about the way Arius presented himself was designed
to create a specific first impression. Here, it said, is a wise man
who knows his stuff.

The Church historian Sozomen says that Arius was involved
in the Melitian schism, a breakaway group in the Alexandrian
church that formed during the worst days of the persecutions.
But Sozomen might have been confused: Arius was a common
name, and Sozomen might have mixed our Arius up with a different one.[3]

It's possible that Arius was a candidate for bishop of Alexandria in 313. If so, he was defeated by Alexander. This might

---

[1] Epiphanius, *Panarion* 69.3.
[2] Rowan Williams, *Arius: Heresy and Tradition* (Grand Rapids, MI: Eerd-
mans, 2002), 32.
[3] Williams, *Arius*, 35–39, 286n79.

explain why Arius later seemed to treat Alexander with patronizing intellectual contempt. At any rate, sometime around 318 Arius and Alexander had a big disagreement over the status of the Son of God in Christian theology, and soon Arius' supporters began meeting in separate Arian groups.

The Church in Alexandria was used to priests acting with a fair amount of independence from their bishop, who was treated as the first among equals. But this was taking priestly independence a bit too far.

WHAT ARIUS TAUGHT

The main point of Arius' teaching was that the Son is subordinate to the Father. Only God, he taught, is unbegotten. God's first creation was the Son, who thus had a beginning and is not eternal in the same way as the Father. The Son is perfect, unalterable, and heir of the Father—but only by the Father's willing gift.[4] He cannot really comprehend the Father.[5]

All this came up because Bishop Alexander had been preaching on the unity of the Holy Trinity, and Arius—who was very proud, it seems, of his philosophical education—thought Alexander had botched it. Yet, Alexander was only teaching what the Church had always believed: that the Father is God, and the Son is God, and the Holy Spirit is God, and that all three of these persons, though each one is distinct, make up only one God.

Arius, applying what he thought was philosophical logic, thought this traditional view was not clearly thought out. And his ideas about the Son had some clear consequences:

---

[4] Williams, *Arius*, 98.
[5] Williams, *Arius*, 63.

1. God is not Father by nature, because there was a time before he became a Father.
2. The Son is not *true* God: he is God only by the Father's grace.
3. The three members of the Trinity are not at all equal: the Son is inferior to the Father by an infinity of glories.[6]

From our modern Catholic point of view, we can see immediately where Arius went wrong. He and his followers assumed that one God meant that the Father was the "original" God, and therefore when we call the Son "God," we're really giving him a kind of courtesy title. A Catholic today would say that the Father, Son, and Holy Spirit have always existed together as God, but Arius assumed the priority of the Father without even realizing that he was making an assumption.[7] Thus Arius always used "God" and the "Father" as interchangeable terms. If you thought any other way, Arius believed, you were lapsing into polytheism.

Arius referred to Proverbs 8:22 as one of his most important proof texts:

The LORD created me at the beginning of his work,
　　the first of his acts of old.

This, according to Arius, referred to the Son, and it meant that there was a time when the Son was not. That became the slogan of Arius and his followers: "There was a time when he was not."

---

6 Williams, *Arius*, 100–103.
7 Williams, *Arius*, 156.

A Big Stink

What was so shocking about Arius' teachings was that they went against the traditional practice of the Church—never mind the doctrine. Christians worship Christ as God. They baptize in the name of the Father, Son, and Holy Spirit. These things imply certain assumptions about the triune nature of God that Arius' interpretation denies and defies.

The true doctrine of the Christian Church was already expressed in the liturgy. But now Arius was calling it into question, and it would have to be defined in theology.

The Church in Alexandria was already a mess. Rowan Williams, in a unique turn of phrase, calls it "spectacularly fissiparous"—meaning that it was always throwing off splinter sects that fought noisy battles with the main Church.[8] Most of these were small minorities, although the Melitian schism had been big enough to be a source of perennial worry. Even that, however, was a local Alexandrian problem. And so Arius might have remained, if it hadn't been for the ambitious Bishop of Nicomedia, a man named Eusebius.

Eusebius of Nicomedia was a man who was going places. At least, he was going places if he had anything to say about it. He had been bishop of the little backwater town of Berytus, but he had wangled a transfer to Nicomedia, the imperial capital of the East—even though canon law at the time prohibited a bishop from leaving his see. Once he had established himself right next door to the emperor, there was really only one bishop who was arguably more powerful in the whole eastern half of the empire: the Bishop of Alexandria, Alexander.

---

[8] Williams, *Arius*, 46.

If Eusebius could make life difficult for Alexander, then who would be the most powerful bishop in the East? After all, it was a new world. Christianity was legal and prosperous now. The Western emperor, Constantine, was a Christian himself, and the Eastern emperor, Licinius, at least had to tolerate Christians or risk the displeasure of the plainly more powerful Constantine. If Christianity was now part of the regular political scene in the empire, shouldn't the bishop in the emperor's own city have precedence? So Eusebius supported Arius in order to instigate his own rise in power above Alexander.

In 319, a year after his first big public disagreement with Arius, Alexander wrote a letter warning about the rapid spread of this new false teaching. And, although Arius was the origina-tor of it, Alexander had no doubt about who was responsible for spreading it far and wide.

> But since Eusebius who is now in Nicomedia thinks he runs the whole Church just because he left his duties in Berytus and took over the church in Nicomedia without any consequences, and since he's put himself up as leader of these apostates, and has even dared to send letters of recommendation hither and yon for them. . . . I didn't think I could keep silent any longer.[9]

Alexander had excommunicated Arius from the church in Alexandria, but Arius (like Origen before him) seems to have ended up in Caesarea, where he rounded up further support from Eastern bishops, including another Eusebius, the famous

---

[9] From a letter of Alexander, quoted in Socrates, *Ecclesiastical History* 1.6.

ARIUS

Church historian of Caesarea.[10] Arius painted himself a poor
wise man who suffered from the abuse of his intellectual inferi-
ors, as he describes himself in a long poem he wrote about his
teachings called the *Thalia*:

> A man much spoken of, who suffers all manner of
>   things for God's glory,
> And, learning from God, I am now no stranger to
>   wisdom and knowledge.[11]

Furthermore, against the authority of his bishop, Arius
opposed the authority of his well-known teachers—easy to do
in the chaotic church of Alexandria, where the authority of the
bishop over priests was often vague. And Alexander, though
he was a competent bishop and an orthodox teacher, was not
the brightest intellectual light in the famously academic city of
Alexandria.

However, Alexander had a secret weapon he was about to
unleash. In about 322, he ordained a brilliant young priest
named Athanasius. From that moment, Eusebius of Nicomedia
and his Arian party would have an opponent whose intellect
nobody could look down on.

By the time Athanasius became a priest, the Arian controversy, as it came to be called, had spread all over the East.
The Pope (in Rome) had been alerted by Alexander and he was
watching with dismay as the whole East seemed to be losing its
marbles.

---

[10] Williams, *Arius*, 53–54.
[11] Quoted in Williams, *Arius*, 85. The passage is preserved in Athanasius,
Three Orations Against the Arians 26.20.44–21.3.

But meanwhile, there were other distractions. The Eastern emperor, Licinius, was becoming increasingly intolerant of Christians, and the Western emperor, Constantine, was becoming increasingly intolerant of Licinius. Eventually, open war broke out between them—a war that Constantine easily won. Now there was just one emperor for the whole Roman Empire, and that emperor was a Christian. And although Constantine stuck to his policy of tolerance for pagans, Jews, and Christians alike, he clearly hoped that Christianity could be the thing that unified his empire.

So he was horrified to find that Christianity itself was in a state of chaos. Arius and his sponsor Eusebius of Nicomedia had made a big stink throughout the Eastern Church and it was even seeping into the West. Constantine would have to do something about this.

And what he did was something really extraordinary.

THE COUNCIL OF NICAEA

In 325, shortly after he defeated Licinius, Constantine called all the bishops in the world to a meeting at Nicaea, not far from the eastern capital of Nicomedia. We don't know precisely how many bishops attended, but it was quite a number. The lowest estimate is about 200; the highest is about 300. So let's call it 250.

What we do know is that Arius' supporters were a small minority. The pro-Arian historian Philostorgius says that 20 bishops on Arius' side attended; but he gives some unlikely names, including one who had been dead for years. Bishops may make extraordinary efforts to attend an important meeting, but death is usually accepted as an excuse. Another historian, Sozomen, says that there were 17 Arians but gives us no names.

Clearly, the vast majority of the bishops in the Empire (and outside it, since even some of those were represented) were traditional Christians who wanted nothing to do with Arius' innovations. And even Arius' supporters were mostly not hardcore supporters, as the results of the Council of Nicaea would prove.

Early in the Council proceedings, a letter from Eusebius of Nicomedia (or possibly of Caesarea—it's sometimes hard to sort out which Eusebius is which) was read to the whole assembly. According to St. Ambrose of Milan, it expressed a fear that the teachings of Alexander would lead to declaring that the Son was of one being—*homoousios* in Greek, or *consubstantialis* in Latin—with the Father. This letter was Eusebius' big mistake. He was already representing the minority party. Now, as Rowan Williams puts it, "Eusebius of Nicomedia, like Arius himself, had rashly begun by stating what his party regarded as non-negotiable.[12]

The great majority of the delegates were horrified by what Eusebius had written. This letter was theatrically torn in pieces in front of the whole assembly.

Meanwhile, Eusebius of Caesarea was trying out the role of peacemaker, and perhaps it was his negotiations that convinced the majority of the pro-Arian bishops to go with the vast majority of the Council. If so, he had more or less completely abandoned Arius, because the Council, in the end, came out with a creed that was worded specifically to include all the phrases Arians

---

[12] Williams, *Arius*, 69.

found completely unacceptable—including saying that the Son was "consubstantial with the Father."

Eusebius of Caesarea seems to have persuaded the vast majority to accept this wording by carefully elucidating the meaning of *homoousios* so that everyone except the most extreme Arians could accept it. All but two of the delegates voted for the final statement of the creed—the first version of what we call the Nicene Creed. Even Eusebius of Nicomedia, who saw which way the wind was blowing, voted for it. Arius was condemned and excommunicated. Constantine immediately exiled him. We note, from our perspective far in the future, that here, for the first time, Constantine decreed a criminal penalty for heresy—a precedent that would create a constant mess in the decades to come.

At some point shortly after the Council of Nicaea, Eusebius of Nicomedia was also exiled. Perhaps he refused to subscribe to the deposition of Arius. Or perhaps he did and then recanted. But Constantine accused Eusebius of Nicomedia of having plotted against him during the war with Licinius, and there may well be some truth to that. Eusebius was an ambitious man and it might have occurred to him that it wouldn't be a bad thing if the emperor right next door owed him a favor or two.

You might think that would be the end of Arius. But you would be very wrong. Eusebius of Nicomedia, in particular, was too wily a politician to let a mere council of the whole Church defeat him. It's hard to tell whether he sincerely believed in what Arius had taught, or whether he just seized on it as a way of furthering his own ambition. But once he had been exiled, the fight was personal.

The Arians Come Roaring Back

The Arians had figured out something about Constantine that perhaps their opponents had not. The thing he most wanted was peace and unity. The Empire had gone through a disastrous period of civil wars before Constantine had finally defeated all the other would-be emperors. There had been enough fighting and wrangling. And in the Church, of all places, shouldn't we be able to find a refuge from all that unpleasantness?

So the Arians, either consciously or instinctively, hit on a devious but very effective strategy. On the one hand, they would proclaim that they had accepted everything in the Council of Nicaea, and then just go on teaching what they had been teaching. On the other hand, when Catholic Christians objected, the Arians would paint them as the enemies of peace and unity.

They got to work very quickly. In 326, the year after the Council, Constantine's mother Helena made a much-publicized pilgrimage to the Holy Land. Eustathius, a prominent anti-Arian bishop there, made some tactless remark about her, and the Arians seized on it, charging him with heresy as well as disrespect. You didn't insult Constantine's mother and get away with it. In 327 Eustathius was deposed and exiled.

That same year, Constantine summoned Arius for a face-to-face meeting. Arius, understanding the emperor's psychology, claimed that he had accepted the Nicene faith, or at least that what he now taught was not contrary to Nicaea, and offered a cagey creed as proof. Constantine saw this as an opportunity to put out all the nasty disputes of the past few years, and perhaps he had a natural impatience with all these Greek subtleties, being a straightforward Westerner himself. He pardoned Arius and recalled him from exile.

But the frail and aging Alexander was not so easily fooled. He could see that Arius was still teaching the same doctrines, and he refused to accept Arius back into communion. And when Alexander died in 328, he was succeeded by his brilliant young protégé Athanasius, who was just as orthodox but had far more brain power to back up his Catholic faith.

Now who was the enemy of peace and unity? It was easy to say, if you were an Arian, that everything would be back to normal if it weren't for that scheming Athanasius. After their disastrous defeat at Nicaea, suddenly the Arians were on the offensive. Eusebius of Nicomedia was back, Arius was back, and they were perfectly willing to get along with everybody, weren't they?

Nevertheless, it was still possible to push things too far. In 332 or 333, Arius wrote to the emperor complaining that no one would receive him in Alexandria. And in this letter Arius pointed out how many supporters he had. This was a big mistake. Constantine's schism alarms went off. The emperor wrote a furious reply, and ordered Arius' works to be burnt, with the death penalty for refusing to turn them over.

It's remarkable how quickly and how craftily the Arians recovered from this setback. In 335 a synod met in Jerusalem on the occasion of the dedication of Constantine's new church there. Arius apparently participated, along with Eusebius of Nicomedia and an honor roll of Athanasius-haters. They condemned Athanasius. Athanasius tried rushing to Constantinople to see Constantine personally, but that was a worse mistake than the one Arius had made. Athanasius ended up in exile—his first exile. (Athanasius almost certainly holds the record for a Christian bishop, with at least five exiles by the traditional count, although you could count several more if you included some of the unofficial running away he had to do.) He was sent to far-off Gaul, where he would be as far as possible from these Eastern theological disputes.

Arius, meanwhile, went back to Alexandria, but it was not a triumphant return. He was greeted with riots in the streets. The Christians of Alexandria, or at least the large orthodox majority, loved their bishop and held Arius responsible for his exile.

The riots angered Constantine again, who was having to spend far too much of his time dealing with theological infighting that an emperor shouldn't have to deal with.

In 336, Constantine interviewed Arius again, who surprised him by assenting to the Nicene Creed as it was written. He wrote it out himself, and swore, "I hold to what I have written."

But there was a story circulating—Athanasius and the historian Socrates Scholasticus both tell it, though Socrates admits it's a rumor—that Arius had really written out a different creed, which he kept concealed in his clothes while he was swearing to Constantine. So he wasn't lying when he said that he held to what he had written, but he was a little coy about what it was he had written.

Not that it did him much good. Just after Arius swore his assent to the Nicene Creed, he died under mysterious circumstances. As the story was told, after Arius met with Constantine, Constantine ordered the orthodox bishop of Constantinople (also named Alexander) to admit Arius to communion the next day. Alexander went to the Church of Holy Wisdom (the old Hagia Sophia, later replaced by the glorious structure that still stands in Istanbul) and prayed that one or the other of them should die before morning—either Arius or Alexander. God decided it should be Arius. While Alexander was praying, Arius had to go to the public rest room, and he died sitting on the toilet.

The story sounds too mean-spiritedly perfect to be true, but it may well have happened that way. It's clear that whatever the circumstances, Arius died quite suddenly. And he was an old man. The circumstances aren't all that mysterious after all: an old man, worn out by years of hardship and stress, has just had the very stressful experience of being summoned to justify himself before the emperor, and perhaps lying to his face. One can imagine how an already frail old man might not survive the experience.

ARIANISM AFTER ARIUS

The Arian movement did not die with Arius. By the time he died, Arius himself had become almost irrelevant to the movement he set in motion. It split and fragmented many ways as it tried to overcome the majority who had condemned it at Nicaea. And very few of the Arians would have consented to call themselves Arians. Many were bishops, and how could a bishop call himself a follower of a simple priest? But for the Catholics, the ones who stuck to the Nicene Creed, "Arianism" became the catchall term for subordinationism, the idea that the Son is inferior to the Father.

It turns out that the Arians, though they never had the majority of ordinary believers, were quite good at getting themselves into positions of power. Constantine's sons, who succeeded him when he died, favored the Arians, and Arian missionaries converted many of the barbarian tribes outside the Roman Empire. It took centuries for the Arian heresy to be overcome.

And it was never really overcome. In fact, you could argue that it continues today as the most powerful and influential of all the Christian heresies. But now it's called Islam.

Islam is, in a way, Arianism taken to its logical conclusion. Like the Arians, Muslims revere Jesus Christ as the Messiah and the greatest of all the prophets. But like the Arians, they insist on the singularity of God the Father. They go further than the Arians in insisting that Jesus is not to be called God at all, and not to be worshipped. But the first steps in that direction were taken by Arius when he insisted that Jesus was called "God" only by the grace of the Father, who was the only true God.

So in fact we could say that Arius died in 336, but the Christian debate with Arianism is still going on today, just as vigorously as ever.

JULIAN THE APOSTATE

CONSTANTINE, THE FIRST Christian emperor, delayed his baptism until he was very near death. He knew that the emperor business was a dirty job, and he was counting on the waters of baptism to wash away the various sins he had to commit to be an effective ruler. When he had his own wife and son executed, for example, it might have shocked a Christian conscience, but for a Roman emperor it was just business as usual. Every emperor had family problems.

But when Constantine's son Constantius came to power, he decided to deal with all his family problems at once. Constantius' cousin Julian was one of these family problems, and years later Julian remembered how Constantius solved problems like him.

> We were closely related—and how this most merciful emperor dealt with us! Without a trial, he executed six of our cousins—mine and his—and my father—his uncle!—and another one of our uncles on our father's side. And he had planned to execute my elder brother

and me as well, but settled for exiling us. He recalled me from that exile, but he took away my brother's title of Caesar just before he murdered him.[1]

This was the Christian family Julian grew up in. This was his earliest impression of what Christianity was all about.

From that kind of Christianity, Julian could find only one refuge. He had the best education available to a young exile in a gilded cage, and he lapped up the wonderful stories of Homer and Hesiod and the other ancient poets like a lost traveler at a desert watering-hole. And those stories started to have an effect on him that no one had predicted.

JULIAN'S BIG SURPRISE

Not surprisingly, Julian, who spent much of his youth far from the madding crowd, grew into an awkward young man. His shoulders were narrow and rounded, and he had a habit of twitching them suddenly as if a bug had landed on him. His head seemed to wobble on his neck and his eyes shifted rapidly, as if he might be scanning for hidden assassins. He seemed a little off-balance when he walked. He tended to look down his nose with what people took for a haughty expression, but then he would suddenly burst into an undignified guffaw if he heard something he thought was funny. He wore a beard, which people made fun of—beards were out of fashion and only stuffy old philosophers wore them.[2] The one life-size statue of Julian that has survived backs up what the ancient writers tell us: it shows a

---

[1] Julian, *Letter to the Athenians* 270.

[2] See: Ammianus Marcellinus, *Res gestae* 22.14; Gregory Nazianzus, *Orations* 5.23.

narrow-shouldered, slightly stooped man with a beard holding a scroll. This is how Julian wanted to be remembered: as a scholar.

Having decided not to murder Julian, Constantius was faced with the problem of what to do with him. Sent away to Gaul with a sharp-eyed minder to take ceremonial command, Julian proved aggravatingly competent. He sorted out long-standing problems in the province and made it run like a well-oiled machine. This was too much for Constantius, who recalled Julian.

But the soldiers had come to like being commanded by someone who was actually good at the job. When the letter came recalling Julian, they surrounded him and declared him emperor.

From that moment, Julian really had no choice. It was a foregone conclusion that Constantius would kill him if he got the chance. Julian would have to fight Constantius and win if he wanted to live any longer.

However, after making preparations for the big civil war, Constantius very conveniently died suddenly. The empire belonged to Julian.

And since he was in charge now, Julian decided he didn't have to pretend any longer. He could tell the world his big secret. He wasn't a Christian at all. Those long hours every day studying the pagan writers, and the example of the most Christian emperor, his cousin, had had their effect. Julian was a worshipper of the old gods.

AGAINST THE GALILEANS

There would be no persecution. Julian wanted that made perfectly clear. But there were going to be some changes made.

The Galileans (as Julian always called the Christians, figuring it would insult them) were not going to have everything their own way any longer. Everyone would be treated equally. But . . .

To start with, Julian decreed that the pagan temples must be restored and repaired. It sounded simple and unobjectionable, but that one simple decree created an unholy mess.

Under Constantine and his sons, many of the temples had been closed and sold off. A few had been turned into churches. Some had become private houses. Others had been demolished, and bricks and stones were always reused, so many a respectable Roman had bits of pagan temple in his garden wall. All those things had been legal and encouraged when they were done. Should a family who had legally bought an old temple for a house now be ruined and thrown out in the street without any compensation? Should new buildings be torn down if they were built with bricks from old temples? And—always an important consideration—how would the mob react when the police came to take away their churches?

Figuring that Christians united might be dangerous to his pagan restoration program, Julian proclaimed universal tolerance for all Christian sects. No longer were Arians and other heretics banned: they could have equal rights with Catholic Christians. It sounded like a very enlightened policy, but Julian was snickering as he considered the probable results. His hope was that the Galileans would beat up on each other and leave him alone.

Relying on Julian's new policy, which recalled all religious exiles from banishment, Athanasius came back to Alexandria from one of his various exiles. But Julian threw him out again as a dangerous rabble-rouser. It was one thing to tolerate different sects among the Christians. It was quite another thing to tolerate strong and able leaders.[3]

Julian also repealed some of the benefits his predecessors had decreed for Christian clergy. Decurions who had become Christian clergy were to resume their secular duties. This was a heavy blow, because the duties of decurions, especially their financial duties, had become ruinously burdensome.

As for religious practice, Julian never forced Christians to worship the pagan gods. But he would often hold his audiences in pagan temples, so that Christians couldn't come without joining in the pagan worship. If you wanted access to the emperor, you had to give up your Galilean superstition.

Soon Julian declared that pagans must be preferred to Christians in government positions. And then he prohibited Christians from practicing law. Now Christians were squeezed out of government, which in imperial days was the main career path for anyone with ambition. Yes, Julian left religion up to everyone's own conscience. But he was making it clear that you couldn't have anything to do with society unless your conscience agreed with his.

Following this, he began reaching beyond the realm of government. Julian banned funerals during daylight hours so that pagans wouldn't have to see any dead bodies. Although Christians celebrated and honored their dead, especially the martyrs, pagans had a superstitious horror of corpses. Christian custom would have to give way to pagan feelings.

Julian's plan was obvious. By treating Christianity as a social disease and quarantining the patients, he wanted to make it impossible for Christians to live as citizens. Anyone with any

---

[3] Julian, *Letters* 51.

drive, anyone who wanted to live as a normal member of society, would have to give up this Galilean foolishness.

The cap on his plan came when he prohibited Christians from having anything to do with teaching. Education was based entirely on the ancient classics, and the ancient writers were all worshippers of the ancient gods. Therefore, Julian pedantically decreed, anyone who taught them without believing in the ancient gods was a liar. And were liars suitable teachers for our children? Certainly not!

Here Julian revealed his real personality. This is exactly the sort of "gotcha" argument your least favorite teacher in grammar school loved. Julian was a pedant through and through: the thing he loved most was being smarter than everyone else in the room.

All this was very distressing to Christians, of course. But it really did pagans no good. Paganism in the Roman Empire was a spent force. It was already dying even before Constantine abandoned it. If Julian really wanted to revive the rotten corpse of paganism, he would have to put some work into it.

THE ANTI-CHURCH

There had never really been a religion called paganism: "pagan" was an insulting term Christians used, a term that meant something like "country bumpkin," because Christianity had taken root most thoroughly in the cities, whereas the old superstitions fed longest in the countryside. Julian always used the term "Hellenes" (the name the Greeks used for themselves) to distinguish his pagan friends from the Galileans. But it was only because of Christianity that he needed such a term at all. In the old days, there had been a bewildering variety of cults. You might worship

Ceres, and I might be a big fan of Apollo, and we could all join together when there was a ceremony in honor of Jupiter Capitolinus. You didn't have to pick one religion and stick with it.

Now Julian wanted to make a pagan religion that was as well organized and as effective as the Christian Church. And to do that, he really had to reinvent paganism from the ground up.

But where would he find a model for that kind of organization?

There was really only one choice. Probably without even thinking about what he was doing, Julian settled on the Church as the model for his new institutionalized pagan religion.

Julian had gotten a glimpse of how demoralized paganism was when he visited Antioch. He let it be known that he was going to visit the famous suburban shrine of Apollo at Daphne, and he expected a big ceremony to be ready, with animals ready to sacrifice and crowds of worshippers to praise the god. Instead, he found one old priest with a goose.[4]

Clearly this pagan revival was going to take some effort.

What made the Christian Church work? Even Julian could see that it was more than just what Christians said. It was what they did. They took care of people—not just the Christian poor, but pagans as well. If you needed help, the Christians didn't ask questions. They just helped. "Why can't we see," he wrote to one of his pagan bishops in Galatia, "that their kindness to strangers, their care for the graves of the dead, and their supposedly holy lives are what really spread this atheism?"[5]

Julian's solution was that his new pagan institutions should be just as charitable as the Christian ones they were designed to

---

4 Julian, *Misopogon* 361–62.
5 Julian, *Letters* 22.

replace. When he was sending supplies for the poor of Galatia, he wrote, "And not just for our people, but for anyone else who needs money." He was going to out-Christian the Christians. "It's a shame that, when no Jew goes a-begging, and the godless Galilean support our poor as well as their own, everyone can see that our people get no help from us."[6]

Here we get a real key to Julian's character. He was a thoroughly Christianized man living in a thoroughly Christianized world. Only fifty years after Constantine had made Christianity legal, the basic assumptions about what piety itself meant had changed permanently. The old pagan world had never worried about the poor; the poor were a nuisance. They were people the gods obviously didn't like much: that was why they were poor. But now it was just obvious to Julian that really good people helped the helpless. Julian's real tragedy was that there was a part of him that was instinctively Christian, and that part looked at the Christians around him and found them not Christian enough.

THE END OF JULIAN

There are some historians who think that Julian was on his way to changing the world. If he had only lived a little longer, he might have rolled back the Christian advances of the past three hundred years and ushered in a glorious new age of revitalized paganism throughout the Mediterranean world.

But probably not. Julian's revived paganism was a zombie, an animated corpse. It took all his attention just to prop it up and give it the illusion of life. However, there might have been

---

6   Julian, *Letters* 49.

a lot more violence if Julian had lived longer. He was already growing tired of the slow pace of the revival and the intransigence of the Christians in the cities. He was already beginning to wink at pagan mobs who lynched Christians they had a grudge against. Things might have gotten much uglier if Julian had had a chance to grow older and more frustrated.

Fortunately he didn't have that chance. Just two years into his reign, he was killed during a daring expedition deep into Persian territory. The rumor that came back from Persia was that his words as he fell from his horse were "You win, Galilean." The story probably isn't true, but it's truer than true. It's one of those legends that sum up a turning point in history in a few short words.

Christians remembered Julian as "the Apostate"—the one emperor who tried to turn back to paganism. There would be no others. From 363 to 1453, when Constantinople finally fell, the Roman Empire would be Christian.

But what can we say about Julian the man? He might have been a very good emperor if he had had better relatives. In spite of his retrograde religious views, he was personally moral—in fact, puritanical—and a competent administrator when the problem was limited and solvable. Perhaps the best tribute to him comes from the Christian poet Prudentius, who neatly summed up Julian in one line:

Faithless he was to God, though not to Rome.[7]

---

7 Prudentius, *Apotheosis*.

Nestorius

Wの SHOULD BE the new archbishop of Constantinople? It was a question with far more than ecclesiastical consequences. Constantinople was the greatest city in the Roman Empire by the year 428, which made the archbishop there second only to the Pope in Rome in his influence. And, really, with the West declining and falling at an alarming rate, the political influence of the man who took over the see in Constantinople would be much greater. How would the clergy and the emperor decide, especially since the church in the city had strong factions, each supporting its own candidate?

You could, of course, pick one of the most eminent thinkers of the age, a man whose flawless erudition and unimpeachable orthodoxy would win all sides and silence all criticism.

Or you could pick some unknown nonentity and hope he wouldn't make waves.

NESTORIUS TAKES CHARGE

Nestorius was that unknown nonentity. He came from Syria, where the locals knew he lived a good Christian life marked by unusual virtue, or at least asceticism. And they said he was a good speaker, and that would help. He wouldn't necessarily make any of the factions in Constantinople happy, but at least they could be satisfied that none of the other factions had gotten what they wanted either. It would be good to have a bishop who wouldn't make waves. Things might calm down for a while.

Then Nestorius arrived. And immediately, on his very first day on the job, he started to make waves.

The emperor's sister, Pulcheria, had dedicated her virginity to Christ, and she had traditionally been allowed the privilege of receiving the Eucharist within the sanctuary—a privilege otherwise reserved for the emperor alone. At the new archbishop's first Mass, she came in with the usual pomp—and he refused to administer the sacrament. This was not a place for a *woman*. And it didn't help when, later on, he made some dismissive remarks about her consecrated virginity. Pulcheria was devoted to the Blessed Virgin Mary, and she thought of herself as emulating that exalted model. And more importantly for Nestorius, she was the one who really ran things in Constantinople. Her brother deferred to her in almost everything. She was not a good enemy to choose if you had to choose an enemy.

Meanwhile, Nestorius' very first homily began with ominous hints of what was to come. The historian Socrates Scholasticus reports his words and the reaction to them:

"Give me the world purged from heretics, emperor, and I will reward you with heaven. Help me get rid of heretics, and I will help you conquer the Persians."

Now the things he said were quite pleasing to some in the crowd, who senselessly hated the mere name "heretic." But (as I said) those who know how to predict a man's character from his expressions did not fail to notice that he had scant brains and a violent and proud disposition.[1]

Was this just hyperbole? No. Right away Nestorius proved he meant what he said about getting rid of the heretics. There was one Arian chapel in Constantinople, which in spite of the laws against heretics had been tolerated because it was doing no harm, and because many of the empire's "barbarian" allies were Arian, so it was helpful that they could see the Arians tolerated when they came for a visit. Nestorius, however, ordered the chapel to be demolished. When they saw the men with axes and sledgehammers, the chapel's congregation set fire to the place rather than give Nestorius the satisfaction of being the one who destroyed it. In the tightly packed city of Constantinople, of course, it was hard to burn just one building, and the fire spread to several others before it was finally put out. Already, Nestorius had caused a minor disaster.

This incident struck the people of the city as a good metaphor for Nestorius' bridge-burning style. Not only the small minority of Arians but also the great majority of orthodox Catholics started to call him the Arsonist—or, as the historian

---

[1] Socrates, *Ecclesiastical History* 7.29.6–7.

John McGuckin translates the breezy Greek term, "Torchie."[2]

And he had only been in office for five days! What would the rest of his term be like?

MOTHER OF GOD

Nestorius seemed to be on a mission to make as many enemies as possible. He next went after the monks, who operated with a great degree of independence. The monks were very popular with the mob and it was probably not a good idea to make them his enemies. But Nestorius seldom stopped to wonder whether his next move was a good idea. He was sure he knew what was right, so he just went ahead and did it.

He quickly offended almost every woman in Constantinople as well. He prohibited women altogether at Vespers, because no decent woman would be out that late, and he seemed to be insulting the empress Pulcheria deliberately. In Nestorius' ideal world, women were silent, subservient, and practically invisible. In Constantinople, and especially in the Church, they had a lot of power and it was not a good idea to make them his enemies. Especially not when the monks already despised him.

It didn't take long for some of his enemies to start plotting their revenge. Some of the monks came to him with a little question—one that was designed to back him into a corner and bring out what they had begun to suspect was Nestorius' real thought on some of the beliefs ordinary Christians most treasured.

We've been having an argument with these other people, the monks explained. *We say that Mary is rightly called Mother*

---

[2] Socrates, *Ecclesiastical History* 7.29.8–9; see also John Anthony McGuckin, *Saint Cyril of Alexandria and the Christological Controversy* (Crestwood, NY: St. Vladimir's Seminary Press, 2004), 24.

of God—in Greek, Theotokos. But these other people say it's not right to call her anything but Mother of the Man—Anthropotokos. Which of us is right?

Nestorius was delighted with the opportunity to show off his erudition. His answer probably struck him as very clever and evenhanded. In a way, he said, you're both right. Each of those names can be used for Mary in a loose and imprecise way. But *technically* the proper term would be Mother of the Christ—*Christotokos.* If you want to be accurate, you'll avoid calling her anything else.[3]

Thus, Constantinople was first introduced to that little word "technically"—in Greek, *akribos*—which the world would soon learn was one of Nestorius' very favorite terms when he was arguing with people. It revealed a lot about the way he thought. The problem with most people, Nestorius seemed to believe, was that they didn't choose their terms carefully enough. When you're talking about important issues of theology, you need to be very precise in your language.

The problem with Nestorius, thought practically everybody else in Constantinople, *was that he had just said Mary wasn't Mother of God.*

The people of the city instantly latched onto that little word "technically" as representing everything they hated about Nestorius. "If Mary is not *technically* the Mother of God," they said, "then her Son is not *technically* God."[4] Mary had always been called Mother of God, as long as anybody could remember. The city—the whole Empire—was devoted to the Blessed Virgin. What was wrong with this new archbishop?

3   McGuckin, *Saint Cyril of Alexandria*, 28.
4   McGuckin, *Saint Cyril of Alexandria*, 28–29.

"He seemed afraid of the word *Theotokos*," Socrates recalled, "as if it were some frightful ghost."[5] In the opinion of Socrates and many others, the problem wasn't loose language on the part of the great majority of Christians. The problem was that Nestorius didn't know what he was talking about. "The baseless fear he showed on this subject merely demonstrated how very ignorant he was. He was naturally a fluent speaker, so people thought he must be well educated. But actually he was disgracefully illiterate." Socrates thought that Nestorius not only didn't know what the great Christian writers before him had written on these subjects, but also didn't care. He was smarter than they were. He could work things out for himself.[6]

Well, if Nestorius didn't know what the great Christians of earlier generations had taught, it was about time somebody told him. Enter the Bishop of Alexandria.

ROME AND ALEXANDRIA ENTER THE FRAY

There was a sort of monkish Internet in those days. As monks traveled around the empire, news could spread amazingly fast. It didn't take long for Nestorius' "technically" to reach almost every church in the East. And thus it came to Alexandria, where it met the man who would become Nestorius' nemesis: Cyril, the Archbishop of Alexandria.

The Bishop of Alexandria was the only one in the East who would be a serious rival to the Bishop of Constantinople. In everyday terms, the one in Alexandria probably had more power: the emperor lived in Constantinople, but the Bishop of

---

[5] Socrates, *Ecclesiastical History* 7.32.
[6] Socrates, *Ecclesiastical History* 7.32.9–10.

Alexandria had taken over much of the administration of his city. He had the power to deal with everything that involved religion—and since pretty much everything involved religion, the Bishop interpreted his powers very widely. In many ways he was more powerful than the imperial governor. And since Alexandria had been a city of mob violence for centuries, with pagan, Christian, and Jewish gangs regularly fighting each other in the streets, Cyril was forced to act almost as a military leader on occasions. On one notorious occasion, the Christian gangs murdered a famous pagan philosopher, Hypatia—almost the only woman in pagan philosophy to achieve a worldwide reputation—and Cyril often still gets the blame for it. It seems, as far as anyone can sort out about what made the mob erupt this time, that they blamed Hypatia for souring relations between Cyril and the Roman governor, who was also a leftover pagan in a Christian world. Sometimes Cyril had more power than he could control.

The news of Nestorius' "technically" deeply worried Cyril. It sounded to him as though the new man in Constantinople was making two Christs—one the man born of Mary, and the other the eternal Word from heaven. That was wrong. There is only one Christ. He had two natures, yes—a human and a divine nature. But you fall into a pit of error if you separate the natures. Mary was mother of the whole Christ, and therefore the Mother of God. To say anything else, as Cyril saw it, was to deny the reality of the Incarnation—of God actually taking on human form to save us.

When the news reached Pope Celestine in Rome, he was just as worried as Cyril was. The two great bishops made common cause; they would have to deal with this error before it spread.

Nestorius, meanwhile, was quite aware of what he saw as plots against him. He seems to have viewed Cyril's dismay at his teaching as simply jealousy of Nestorius' more powerful position. And if Cyril was going to play politics, Nestorius would show he could win that game.

Cyril began an all-out campaign against what he saw as the Nestorian heresy of separating the two natures of Christ. He sent a treatise explaining what had always been Christian doctrine, as Cyril understood it, to the emperor, Theodosius II. And he sent another treatise to the Empress Pulcheria and the imperial ladies, showing that he understood how the imperial palace worked better than Nestorius did.

Yes, Cyril said in these treatises, there are two natures in Christ. Everybody knows that. But you can't separate them. If God as God did not come to be born and die as Jesus Christ, then we are not saved and there is no Christian religion. The Eucharist is the flesh of God—only for that reason can it give us life.

The treatises were well argued and convincing. But it turned out that Cyril had made a tactical error. It was true that Pulcheria and her circle of intelligent aristocratic women had enormous influence over what the relatively weak Theodosius II did and thought. But it was very bad form to point that out. By sending a treatise directly to the ladies, Cyril had insulted Theodosius. For the moment, Nestorius had the advantage. He immediately seized it and began to ask for a synod to be called at Constantinople to decide the question, and doubtless to give his thoughts the official stamp of approval while at the same time heaping anathemas on Cyril. Meanwhile, he began a series of sermons on Christology. In these Nestorius showed that there was no advantage so big that he couldn't squander it.

"Let no one call Mary 'Mother of God,'" he thundered from the pulpit.[7] And it really didn't matter what he said after that. He had lost his audience: a few intellectuals might be able to follow the rest of the argument, but all the ordinary people of the city heard was that he had said Mary wasn't Mother of God. And they had always called her Mother of God. The phrase had been in their prayers for centuries. It was in the hymns they had learned from their grandparents.

It was Nestorius' rhetorical style that doomed him as a preacher. He had no talent for popular communication. His sermons were full of pedantic distinctions and frequently punctuated by that little word "technically," which seemed designed to say that Nestorius thought everyone else was kind of stupid.

On the Sunday before Christmas in 428, Proclus, a bishop without portfolio—he had been consecrated for a see that, disregarding Constantinople's wishes, had picked its own bishop—preached a sermon in the presence of Nestorius himself. His subject was the Virgin Mother of God. The congregation roared with applause. Nestorius was not happy.

It was time, he decided, to show these people who was boss.

The monks began public demonstrations, carrying signs accusing Nestorius of the "two sons" heresy of Paul of Samosata: he was teaching, they said, that Jesus wasn't *technically* God. Nestorius sent the police to arrest and flog one of these pests, but the mob overwhelmed the officials and carried the monk off in a triumphal procession.

Encouraged by their popular support, some of the monks began to heckle Nestorius when he was preaching. He responded

---

[7] Socrates, *Ecclesiastical History* 7.32.

by inviting them to a civilized debate the next day at his palace—and then when they showed up he had them beaten by guards.

Nestorius seemed to think he was showing the city that he was in charge. But the city got the message that he was an ignorant thug. Many of the monks were now refusing to commune with Nestorius, and the Archbishop found himself treated as if he had been excommunicated in his own see.

Nevertheless, Nestorius charged ahead. He chose this moment to interfere in the affairs of Rome and Alexandria, showing that he intended to put even the Pope in his place. There were some priests from Alexandria who had been making complaints about Cyril, and there were some exiles from the West who had been charged with heresy. Nestorius began an investigation into both sets of complaints, showing that he was perfectly willing to act as judge over both Alexandria and Rome. He was aiming at complete control over the whole Christian Church.

Pope Celestine, meanwhile, decided that the time had come to make Nestorius aware that the Church was not going to accept his teaching, He took the extraordinary step of making Cyril responsible, as the pope's representative, for judging the orthodoxy of Nestorius and for setting the conditions under which he could continue as bishop. Clearly, as far as both Cyril and Celestine were concerned, Rome still had the ultimate authority, no matter how much Nestorius might fantasize about being pope himself.

Now Nestorius really had to dig in. Many of his advisers suggested that he should accept Rome's decision, but Nestorius had been kicked in the pride. From the very beginning of his reign, these people had been questioning his authority. Was he going to let them get away with that?

As he was celebrating the liturgy in Constantinople with all the usual pomp, messengers came in from Alexandria. Right in front of the whole congregation, they delivered a long letter from Cyril. At the end of it were twelve headings or "chapters," statements of belief which Nestorius had to sign to prove his orthodoxy. To prove his orthodoxy to whom? The Bishop of Alexandria!

Then Nestorius got some very good news. As he had been requesting, the emperor was going to call a meeting.

And then the news turned very bad. Not only was this going to be a full council of the Church, rather than a small synod of bishops Nestorius thought he could trust, but it was also going to be at Ephesus instead of Constantinople.

Furthermore, Ephesus was the world's chief center of the cult of the Mother of God—the place where, according to tradition, the Virgin Mary had gone to live with the Apostle John.

The Council of Ephesus

It might have been Pulcheria's doing, the historian John McGuckin suggests.[8] As a devoted follower of the Blessed Virgin, Pulcheria had a strong interest in seeing that the Theotokos controversy was resolved against Nestorius, and she had the influence to stack the deck against him.

Theodosius certainly did all he could to make sure it was a proper council and not a riot. Some of the monks were hard to distinguish from gangs of thugs, so Theodosius ordered that they be kept out of Ephesus during the council. None of the bishops would be allowed to run off to Constantinople during

---

8 McGuckin, *Saint Cyril of Alexandria*, 47.

the council and make a separate appeal to the emperor. And there would be troops to keep order, under the command of one of Theodosius' most trusted men.

But Theodosius couldn't take everything into account. For a start, the soldiers he sent arrived with Nestorius, and their commander was one of Nestorius' most ardent supporters. The impression it created was that Nestorius had arrived with his own goon squad to force the bishops to decide things his way. And no bishop likes being forced to do anything.

On the other side, the soldiers might keep out wandering monks, but there was still the local mob to deal with. Ephesus, the city where Mary had spent her last years with the Apostle John, was fanatically proud of its association with the Blessed Virgin, and anyone who spoke a word against the Mother of God was looking for a black eye.

Things didn't start well for Nestorius. Memnon, Archbishop of Ephesus, refused communion to Nestorius but welcomed Cyril and his many Egyptian bishops enthusiastically. They came in with what was practically a ticker-tape parade, and that couldn't have put Nestorius in a good mood. Nestorius had hoped to make the council a trial of Cyril, but it seemed to be evolving into a trial of Nestorius instead.

The Palestinian bishops also immediately allied themselves with Cyril. Nestorius hoped for some support from Syria, but they were delayed by bad weather and bad luck. As for the West, there was not much representation at all. The Western Empire was busy declining and falling. It had been expected that St. Augustine would be one of the leading thinkers at the council, but he had already died during the Vandal invasion of Africa. Of course it was already known that the Pope was on Cyril's side.

So Nestorius was down on his luck. But even if he hadn't found misfortune ready-made, he was perfectly capable of making his own. Nestorius was his own worst enemy. He blundered this way and that, alienating potential allies and infuriating the mob. Meeting individually with undecided bishops before the council opened, he managed to convert almost every one of them into an enemy. For someone who liked to insist on precise language, he could be appallingly vague. "We must not call the one who became man for us God," he said to one of the bishops. And, "I refuse to acknowledge as God an infant of two or three months old!"[9] It may be that he was trying to argue for a precise distinction of the natures in Christ. But it's no wonder that bishops walked out of meetings with him holding their heads and gasping, "Nestorius just denied the Incarnation!"[10]

It didn't help anybody's mood that Ephesus was a rotten place to hold a council in the summer. Ephesus was hot beyond endurance—literally beyond endurance in some cases, since we hear that some of the elderly bishops died while waiting for the council to open. And Bishop John of Antioch and his Syrian delegation still hadn't shown up.

The Emperor's instructions were clear: there were to be no excuses for showing up late. Nevertheless, the council was delayed by sixteen days while everyone waited for the Syrians. Cyril finally decided to open the council anyway, with himself as president.

There was just one problem. The council could not begin legally until the emperor's order convening it was read in the presence of the assembly. And Candidian, the man in charge of

9 McGuckin, *Saint Cyril of Alexandria*, 64.
10 Socrates, *Ecclesiastical History* 7.32.

the soldiers, had also been put in charge of the emperor's order. He was a firm ally of Nestorius and insisted that the meeting was not to begin until he said so. Storming into the assembly with his soldiers, he demanded that the bishops disperse. His instruction from the emperor, he said, did not allow him to let this illegal partisan assembly continue.

The bishops looked around. There were at least two hundred of them. Only about thirty Nestorius loyalists were missing, plus the dozen or two who were still on their way from Syria. This was a partisan meeting?

We don't believe you, various bishops told Candidian. *This is just you bluffing. How do we know what's in those orders? You're probably just making it up.*

Furious, Candidian opened the emperor's order and read it in front of the assembly. And it wasn't until he had finished and looked up with a smile of smug satisfaction that he realized the awful mistake he had made. The order had been read in the presence of the assembly. The council was now in session.

Candidian withdrew in a huff. Cyril and the rest got on with the business at hand. The propositions of Nestorius were read, and various bishops he had talked to in the past few days recounted how he had denied the Incarnation. Nestorius was condemned and deposed as bishop.

We'll let Cyril himself describe what happened next.

The entire population of the city stood from dawn to dusk waiting for the decision of the holy council. When they heard that the wretched man was deposed, they all began, with one voice, to cry out in praise of the holy council, glorifying God because the enemy of the faith had fallen. When we came out of the church they made a procession ahead of us to the lodging house (for it was getting dark by this time) and even the women came out carrying incense to perfume the path before us.[11]

So, said Cyril to his correspondent back home, all we have to do is finish the formal paperwork excommunicating Nestorius, and I'll be back home with you in no time.

That turned out to be an optimistic estimate.

Candidian, still fuming, refused to acknowledge that an official council had taken place. And since it hadn't taken place, the bishops couldn't leave. He told his soldiers to make sure they all stayed in Ephesus.

Cyril, meanwhile, managed to sneak a messenger out with a summary of the council's proceedings to be taken to the emperor in Constantinople. Nestorius also sent a message back to the capital complaining of the illegal partisan assembly that had usurped the place of the real council.

And then came the Syrians.

When John of Antioch arrived, he was furious that the council had gone ahead without him and his party. He allied himself with Nestorius, and all of Nestorius' allies—forty-three of them—held their own council, which they insisted was the real Council of Ephesus. They excommunicated all two hundred bishops at Cyril's council.

Meanwhile, the news was coming back to Constantinople. Cyril had made sure his version of the council's decisions would be heard all over the city, and there were celebrations in the streets when the ordinary citizens heard that Nestorius, the

---

[11] Cyril of Alexandria, *Letters* 24.

enemy of the Theotokos, was deposed. But when Theodosius received the conflicting reports of the council from Candidian, from Nestorius, and from John of Antioch's mini-council, he was at best puzzled. It had seemed that he was ready to accept the larger council's verdict, but now he wasn't sure. Who was right? Which was the real Council of Ephesus?

Seeing the emperor wavering, the monks of Constantinople organized an extraordinary procession. They marched to the palace to plead with the emperor to accept the original council's verdict. And marching at their head was the ancient holy monk Dalmatius—a man whom the emperor had once begged to take on the job of Archbishop of Constantinople, but who had refused because he had taken an extreme vow. It was an age when holy men went to extremes, and Dalmatius had stayed in his cell without coming out for forty-six years. But now, here he was marching through the streets. That was how important the Mother of God question was to the monks.

Theodosius was impressed. But he also had the letters from Candidian and Nestorius, and the decision of John of Antioch's counter-council to take into account.

And so he came to a decision that was typical of him. He decisively refused to make a decision. He accepted the results of both councils. Everybody was excommunicated—Cyril, Nestorius, Memnon, the whole lot of them. Problem solved.

Of course it solved nothing. Delegates from the Pope in Rome finally arrived at Ephesus and confirmed Cyril's council, but Candidian was still refusing to admit that the council had taken place. He began to deal with the problem as a military operation, besieging the bishops in the city, cutting off their supplies, and trying to starve them into submission. More of the older bishops died in the sweltering city.

But by now the real battle was in Constantinople, where Cyril's allies out-organized and out-bribed Nestorius and his proxies. (Bribery sounds very sordid to us, but it was more or less the official way of getting things done in Constantinople at the time. If you made a request, a gift was accepted and expected.)

Most of all, though, Theodosius felt the constant pressure of public opinion. A stronger or stupider emperor might have ignored what the people thought, but Theodosius was neither strong nor stupid. He could see that the people were devoted to the Mother of God. He could see that the holy men he sincerely admired, like Dalmatius, were on the side of the people. In the end, Nestorius stayed deposed, but Cyril and Memnon resumed their sees. Theodosius mostly accepted the majority position at Ephesus.

Nestorius was at first allowed to retire, but when he still wouldn't stop issuing pamphlets about what was *technically* wrong with the emperor's decision, he was exiled to the isolated city of Petra, and then finally to the Great Oasis in Egypt, which was surrounded by so many miles of desert that it had become a dumping ground for the most embarrassing political exiles. On the way, Nestorius endured some remarkable *Arabian Nights* adventures, being captured by desert bandits and held for ransom, all of which he recounted in an autobiography which is usually known as the *Book of Heracleides* but might also have been titled *Poor Me*.

After the Council of Ephesus, long and patient diplomacy finally reconciled Cyril with John of Antioch and most of the Syrians. But there were still some allies of Nestorius in the East who never accepted his deposition. The Catholic and Orthodox churches referred to these eastern groups as "Nestorians," and they still exist today—but they'd rather you didn't call them

Nestorian. In 1994, Pope John Paul II and Patriarch Dinkha IV of the Assyrian Church of the East signed a Common Christological Declaration. In it the Assyrian Church recognized the validity of the term *Theotokos* and acknowledged the tradition of Petrine primacy. Since then, the two churches have agreed to communion in times of necessity for each other's followers, and although the Assyrians don't accept the Council of Ephesus or any of the ecumenical councils after it, the Catholic Church accepts their teaching as consistent with Catholic theology.

In fact, some scholars hold that the "Nestorian" churches were never theologically Nestorian. They were rather Persian and anti-Byzantine. Jacob of Serugh and other later East Syrian Fathers are today commonly revered as Fathers by the Catholic Church.

In other words, it may be that, *technically*, the only real Nestorian was Nestorius.

INFAMY'S LAST WORDS

✥

V ILLAINY IS HARDLY a matter of the distant past. Nestorius was not the end of the drama. The Church today still
suffers the worst from traitors within and persecutors without.

Bishops in the twenty-first century are certainly more cau-
tious and circumspect about their condemnations than were
some of their predecessors in the second and fourth centuries.
They're less likely to hurl invective and more likely to carry on
a private correspondence with public sinners in their purview,
calling them to repentance without calling them names.

Why the change? Do clergy today lack something that
clergy had in the primitive Church? Probably not. Remember
that many of the villains in this book were clergymen. History
preserves the memory of villains as it preserves the memory of
heroes. Most of the clergy, like most of us generally, just get
through their days doing a job (or not doing it) without attract-
ing the attention of the chroniclers.

What's changed, perhaps, is the *shock value* of treachery,
immorality, and ferocious persecution. To be deep in history is

to know that scandal is a constant. To be deep in history is to know that persecution waxes and wanes on the earth, but that it never quite goes away. The Master predicted that Christians would always live with scandals and always live with persecution (but woe to those who cause scandal, he said, and woe to the persecutors). The Apostles struggled against heresy and perfidy, and they knew that these problems would plague their successors as well.

By the middle of the fifth century, the Church had seen it all and survived—and prevailed over it. Most of our modern, enhanced, supercharged heresies are actually unoriginal. The ideas may have taken Paul and Peter by surprise, and Irenaeus and Athanasius. But they shouldn't surprise us today.

Nor should they shake our faith. Long ago, the Lord promised to make a "footstool" of the enemies of his Son (see Psalm 110:1). Third-century Christians saw this promise fulfilled as the persecuting Emperor Valerian was defeated in battle by Shapur, a Persian: Shapur used his vanquished enemy's back for a boost when mounting his horse. After a while, Shapur grew tired of the game and had Valerian made into a plush toy to adorn the walls of a temple.

But God doesn't only make our enemies into footstools. He oftentimes makes them into friends. Sometimes we win not only our intellectual arguments with persecutors and heretics; we win their hearts as well. This is what we should always strive to do.

Continuing on, we should bear in mind the story of Saul of Tarsus, who once breathed murderous threats against the Church, and then became its greatest champion.

Our enemies should sharpen us. And we should sharpen them, too, as we bring them to the truth of Jesus Christ.